SOCIAL RESEARCH

USING MICROCASE

Lynne Roberts

MICROCASE CORPORATION

Michael Corbett

BALL STATE UNIVERSITY

Editor	David Smetters
Production Supervisor	Jodi Gleason
Design & Production	Michael Brugman Design
Copy Editor	Margaret Moore

IBM PC and IBM PC DOS are registered trademarks of International Business Machines, Inc.

ShowCase and *MicroCase* are registered trademarks of MicroCase Corporation.

Printed in the United States of America

1 2 3 4 5 6 7 8 9 10–98 97 96

Contents

About the Authors

Lynne Roberts received her Ph.D. from Stanford University where she also was on the staff of the Computing Center. She left Stanford to inaugurate a year-long research methods course in the then-new doctoral program offered by the School of Social Welfare at the University of California, Berkeley. After several years, she joined the faculty of the University of Washington in Seattle where she served as Associate Professor of Sociology. In 1984, she left academic life to pursue her interests in educational software. Currently, she is president of MicroCase Corporation. During her tenure at Washington, Roberts taught statistics at both the undergraduate and graduate levels. Trained as an experimental social psychologist, she designed and conducted many experiments, the results of which she reported in a book and a number of scholarly articles. She also has published articles on methodological subjects including scaling and experimental design.

Michael Corbett received his Ph.D. from the University of Iowa. He is now professor of political science at Ball State University, where he teaches courses covering an introduction to political science, research methods in political science, and public opinion. He is author of numerous scholarly articles and of three books: *Political Tolerance in America: Freedom and Equality in Public Attitudes* (New York: Longman, 1982), *American Public Opinion: Trends, Processes, and Patterns* (New York: Longman, 1991), and *Research Methods in Political Science: An Introduction Using MicroCase* (Bellevue: MicroCase, 1996).

Introduction

This workbook is about *doing* social research. There is nothing make-believe about what you will be doing. You'll use the same resources and techniques used by professional social science researchers.

Since the exercises differ in length and difficulty, your instructor may assign only selected questions, or you may be given alternative questions. Be sure to carefully check any information from your instructor so that you will do the appropriate problems. Some of the problems will ask you to print certain results and attach them to your worksheet. If you do not have a printer or you have been instructed not to use a printer, simply complete the written exercises.

Many of the exercises will have a variety of possible answers. This reflects the nature of research—there is no "correct" way to do research. In most situations, a variety of approaches are equally appropriate.

The exercises are designed so that the introductory material does not require a computer. If your computer time is limited, you may read this material beforehand and save your computer time for completing the worksheets. In any case, you should carefully read the introductory material before starting on the written exercises.

GETTING STARTED

After your computer has booted up, follow these instructions:

- Place the diskette in the A or the B drive.

- Switch to the drive (A or B) that has the diskette in it; to do this *type* **A:** (or **B:**) and then *press <ENTER>*.

- When the DOS prompt (i.e., A:> or B:>) for that drive is on the screen, *type* **MC** and *press <ENTER>*.

- It will take from 20 seconds to a minute for the program to load, depending on the speed of your computer. The first time you start Student MicroCase, you will be asked to type in your name. It is very important that you type your name correctly, since your name and the date will appear on all printed output from Student MicroCase. *Press <ENTER>* after you type your name; if your entry is correct, *press <ENTER> again* in response to the next prompt. The title screen will appear.

- After you have read the title screen, *press <ENTER>* to begin. MicroCase works from two primary menus. If you are using a color monitor, the first menu is blue and the second menu is red. The first menu—the blue menu—will now be on the screen.

Introductory Exercise: Exploring Data Files

OVERVIEW

In this introductory exercise, you will discover how easy it is to use MicroCase to explore two of the data files that you will be using throughout this workbook. You will see how to use MicroCase to do such tasks as

- open a data file;
- obtain an on-screen list of the variables in the data file;
- view the description of any particular variable;
- use the easy and powerful search feature to find any variables that contain a certain word or phrase; and
- select a variable for analysis.

BASICS OF MICROCASE

This exercise introduces the MicroCase software and databases—there is no corresponding chapter in the textbook. You may complete this exercise before you begin reading the textbook.

Start MicroCase following the directions in "Getting Started." The **DATA AND FILE MANAGEMENT** menu should be on the screen. It looks like this:

```
┌─────────────────────────────────────────────────────────────────┐
│                   DATA AND FILE MANAGEMENT                        │
│───────────────────────────────────────────────────────────────── │
│ S. Switch to STATISTICAL ANALYSIS MENU                            │
│                                                                   │
│   DATA MANAGEMENT:                                                │
│      A. Define Variables/Recodes      E. Codebook                 │
│      B. Collapse/Strip Categories     F. Edit Variable Information │
│      C. Enter Data from Keyboard      G. Grading Recode           │
│      D. List or Print Variable Values H. Setup Data Entry         │
│                                                                   │
│   FILE MANAGEMENT:                                                │
│     *I. Open, Look, Erase or Copy File  M. Move Data between Files │
│     *J. Create New Data File            N. Merge Files            │
│      K. Create Subset File              O. Create Aggregation File │
│      L. Import/Export Data              P. Create Statistical Summary │
│                                                                   │
│  *X. EXIT from MicroCase                                          │
└─────────────────────────────────────────────────────────────────┘
```

Notice that certain tasks are in bold and have an asterisk to the left of them. These are the tasks that are currently available for use in Student MicroCase. When you first start, only three tasks are available: You may open a data file, create a data file, or exit from MicroCase. After you open a data file, other tasks will be available. The specific tasks will depend on the particular data file you're using.

When you first start MicroCase, the highlight is on **I. Open, Look, Erase or Copy File.** *Press <ENTER>* to select this task. You can see that there are seven data files available: **SURVEY, USA, EXPER, TEST, US&DC, CONTENT**, and **CATI**.

Using the **arrow** keys to move the highlight, place it on **USA** and *press <ENTER>*. This screen gives you basic information about the data file. We can see that this file is based on the 50 states (or cases) and includes 129 variables.

A variable is anything that varies among the objects being examined. Since we are dealing with states, a variable in this data file would be things that vary across states. For example, the crime rate is one such variable. Church membership rate, voter participation rate, population, and geographic area are other variables included in this data file. In this course, we'll spend quite a bit of time talking about variables, how to create them, and how to use them. Let's examine the variables in this data set.

Press the **F3** function key. Function keys are located at either the top or the left of your keyboard. Two windows will open on the screen. They look like this:

```
┌─────────────────┐
│1) Case ID       │
├─────────────────┤
│ 2)  POP 1990    │
│ 3)  POP GO 90   │
│ 4)  % WHITE     │
│ 5)  % BLACK     │
│ 6)  % ASIAN     │
│ 7)  %N.AMERICA  │
│ 8)  % HISPANIC  │
│ 9)  MEXICAN K   │
│10)  P.RICAN K   │
│11)  CUBAN K     │
│12)  IMMIGRANTS  │
│13)  AGE 5-17    │
│14)  % OVER 65   │
│15)  AVER. AGE   │
│16)  % RURAL     │
│17)  % METROPOL  │
└─────────────────┘
```

```
┌────────────────────────────────────────┐
│ ↑, ↓, PgUp,PgDn,Home,End: Scroll List   │
│ ─→ :Examine Variable Description         │
│ A:Alphabetic Order                       │
│ G:Goto…                                  │
│ S:Search for…                            │
│                                          │
│ Press <ENTER> to Close Window            │
└────────────────────────────────────────┘
```

The window on the left presents a list of names and numbers of all the variables in the **USA** data file. This is called the *codebook window*. Note that the first variable is highlighted. This is variable number 1 and its name is Case ID—generally in the workbook, variables will be identified by both their name and number: 1) Case ID. You may use the up and down arrow keys, the page up and page down keys, and the home and end keys to move through the list. Place the highlight on **37) WARM WINTR** and *press* the **right arrow** key. A new window will open giving the description of the variable that is highlighted—AVERAGE JANUARY LOW TEMPERATURE. *Press* the **down arrow** key. The description of the next variable now appears in the window. You may examine the description of any variable in the **USA** data file using this feature. *Press <ENTER>* to close the description window. *Press <ENTER> again* to close the codebook window.

Press <ENTER> to return to the main menu. The available tasks have now been changed and the highlight is on the first menu line, **S. Switch to Statistical Analysis Menu.** *Press <ENTER>.* You are now on the second main menu for MicroCase, the **STATISTICAL ANALYSIS** menu. This menu is red and it looks like this:

```
┌─────────────────────────────────────────────────────────────────┐
│                    STATISTICAL ANALYSIS                           │
│  ───────────────────────────────────────────────────────────     │
│                                                                   │
│  *S. Switch to DATA AND FILE MANAGEMENT MENU                      │
│                                                                   │
│     BASIC STATISTICAL ANALYSIS:                                   │
│        *A. Univariate Statistics        *F. Scatterplot           │
│         B. Tabular Statistics           *G. Correlation           │
│         C. Analysis of Variance          H. Partial Correlation   │
│         D. Covariance Analysis          *I. Regression            │
│        *E. Mapping Variables                                      │
│                                                                   │
│     ADVANCED STATISTICAL ANALYSIS:                                │
│         J. Regression Models             L. Factor Analysis       │
│         K. Curve Fitting                 M. Logistic Regression   │
│                                          N. Time Series           │
│                                                                   │
│     Q. Interactive Batch                                          │
│                                                                   │
│  *X. Exit from MicroCase                                          │
│                                                                   │
│                                            OPEN FILE:USA          │
└─────────────────────────────────────────────────────────────────┘
```

Again look at the items in bold type with the asterisks. Only these tasks are available in Student MicroCase with the **USA** data file. Let's look at the mapping task.

To select mapping, *press* **E** (or place the highlight on **E. Mapping Variables** and *press <ENTER>*). You are now asked for the name or number of the variable to be mapped.

Type **72** and *press <ENTER>.* A map of the United States appears on your screen and is also shown in Figure 1.1. The full description of the variable is

shown at the bottom of the map: 1990: NUMBER OF RESIDENTS WHO PUR-
CHASED HUNTING LICENSES PER 1,000 POPULATION (U.S. FISH &
WILDLIFE). This map shows the hunting license rate for each state. Notice that
the states appear in five different colors, from very dark to very light. The darker
the state, the higher the hunting license rate. Not surprisingly, the states with the
best opportunities for hunting tend to have the highest rates.

A menu with various options is shown on the bottom of the screen. Let's
explore some of these options. *Type* **N** *(for Name)*. The state with the highest value
changes color and is marked by an arrow. In the lower left corner of the screen,
the name of this state appears—Idaho. The hunting license rate for Idaho was
586.4—out of every 1,000 residents, 586.4 purchased hunting licenses in 1990.
Press the **down arrow** key to move to the next highest state. Now the screen
shows that North Dakota was second with a rate of 575.3. If you keep pressing the
down arrow, you will be able to see the hunting license rate for each state.

Figure 1.1   1990: Number of residents who purchased hunting
licenses per 1,000 population (U.S. Fish & Wildlife)

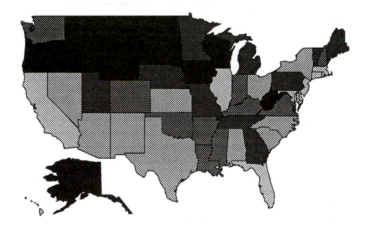

To see all 50 states ranked from high to low, simply *type* **D** *(for Distribution)*.
Here you can see that Hawaii is lowest with a rate of 11.7, and Rhode Island is
next lowest with a rate of 20.0. *Press <ENTER>* to return to the map. *Press* **L** *(for
Legend)*. You can see the map legend—that is, the values associated with each
color. States with 254.2 to 586.4 are in the highest group, while states with rates
from 11.7 to 57.2 are in the lowest group.

Press **S** *(for Spot)*. Each state is now represented by a spot. The size of the
spot is determined by the relative magnitude of the value for each state. Idaho
and North Dakota have large spots, while Hawaii and Rhode Island have very

small spots. *Press <ENTER>* to return to the beginning of the task.

Let's look at the map of another variable; this time, let's use the variable name rather than the variable number. *Type* **PICK** and *press <ENTER>*. (We do not need to type the full name, only enough letters to uniquely identify the variable.) The map of pickups per 1,000 now fills in. *Press* **N** (for Name) and we can see that Idaho is the highest state with a rate of 363.6. This isn't much of a surprise. In fact, the map of pickup trucks looks very similar to the map of hunting licenses (see Figure 1.2). *Press* **D** (for Distribution) to see the entire distribution. Connecticut is lowest with 36.3, and New Jersey is next lowest with 43.8. *Press <ENTER> twice* to return to the prompt for a new variable to be mapped.

Figure 1.2   1989: Light trucks (pickups) per 1,000 (Highway)

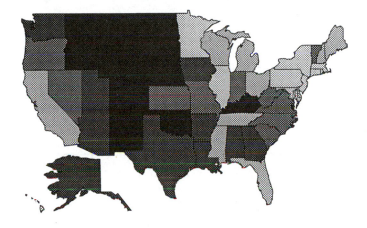

We also can select a variable using the codebook window. *Press* the **F3** function key. Place the highlight on **37) WARM WINTR** and *press* the **left arrow** key. Notice that a check mark appears next to the name of the variable. This indicates that you have selected the variable for analysis. (If you change your mind, you may erase this mark by pressing the left arrow key a second time.) To complete your selection of the variable WARM WINTR, and to close the codebook window, *press <ENTER>*. See Figure 1.3.

Figure 1.3   Average January low temperature

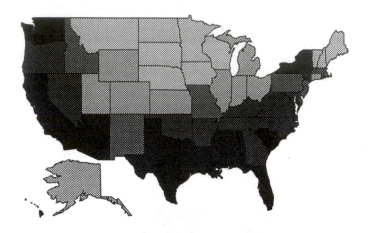

This is a map of the average low temperature in January. This map is almost exactly the opposite of the map of hunting license rates. Not too surprising—the best opportunities for hunting tend to be in the colder states. *Press* **D** (for Distribution). Hawaii is the warmest with an average January low of 65, while North Dakota is the coldest with an average low of –3 degrees.

We now have three different ways of selecting variables for use in a task: We can use the variable number, we can use the variable name, or we can use the F3 key.

MicroCase also provides an easier means of comparing two maps. *Press* **S** (for Spot). *Press* **C** (for Compare). The map is now redrawn using only the top half of the screen and you are prompted for a second variable. *Type* **72** and *press* <ENTER>. You can now compare the map of winter temperatures with the map of the hunting license rate. See Figure 1.4. *Press* <ENTER> *three times* to return to the beginning of the task.

Figure 1.4   Comparison of 37) WARM WINTR and 72) HUNTING

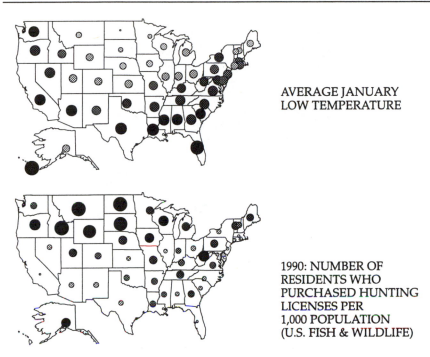

AVERAGE JANUARY
LOW TEMPERATURE

1990: NUMBER OF
RESIDENTS WHO
PURCHASED HUNTING
LICENSES PER
1,000 POPULATION
(U.S. FISH & WILDLIFE)

Let's look at one last map before we leave this data file. *Type* **%NO RELIG.** and *press <ENTER>*. The map of the percent of the population claiming no religion now appears; see Figure 1.5. Notice that on this map Alaska and Hawaii are a different color; *press* **D** (for Distribution) to see the distribution. They both have a value of –99 on this variable. That means that data were not available for these two states on this variable. Only 48 states have valid data on the rate of nonreligious individuals. The state with the highest rate of persons without a religion is Oregon with a rate of 17.2 percent—17.2 per 100 claim to have no religion. The state with the lowest rate of nonreligious individuals is North Dakota with 1.6 percent.

Figure 1.5   1990: Percent of the population who say they have no religion (Kosmin)

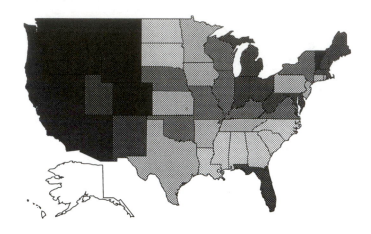

Press *<ENTER> as many times as necessary* to return to the **STATISTICAL ANALYSIS** menu. You also may return to the main menu by pressing the **<ESC>** key, *typing* **Y** in response to the prompt, and *pressing <ENTER>*—you may use this procedure to return to the main menu at any time. *Press* **S** (or place the highlight on the top line and *press <ENTER>*). You are now back on the first menu. Let's now take a look at a different kind of data set, one based on responses from individuals. *Press* **I**. Now highlight the file named **SURVEY** and *press <ENTER>*.

These data are from the 1993 General Social Survey conducted by NORC. There were 1,606 respondents (or cases), and this data file contains a selection of 153 variables from that survey. Let's look at some of the variables in this data file. *Press* the **F3** key. After the window opens, *press* the **right arrow** key. The first variable is the respondent's sex. When the categories of a variable are labeled, these labels also are shown in the description window. There are two categories of the variable sex: male and female.

Use the **up** and **down arrow** keys to scroll through the descriptions of the variables. Some of these variables relate to characteristics of the respondent, such as sex, age, and race. These are called *demographic* characteristics. Other variables are about behaviors and attitudes, such as voting behavior, attitudes toward abortion, and favorite activities. Notice that the variables in this data set are based on individuals rather than on geographic areas. *Press <ENTER> twice* to close the description and the codebook windows.

Press <ENTER> twice again to go to the **STATISTICAL ANALYSIS** menu. Notice that there is no asterisk beside the mapping task with this data file—obviously, mapping individuals makes no sense. So we will have to find another technique for looking at these data. *Type* **A** to select **A. Univariate Statistics**. (*Uni* is a Latin prefix meaning "one." So this task is simply "one variable" analysis.)

Type **SEX** and *press <ENTER>*. *Press <ENTER>* a second time when asked about a subset. A pie chart appears. The legend for the pie colors is shown at the left. See Figure 1.6.

Figure 1.6   Pie chart showing the distribution of 1) SEX

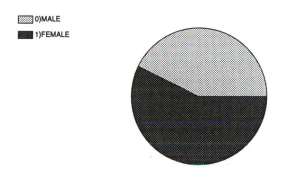

We can see that the slice of the pie representing females is larger than the slice representing males. (In Chapter 4, we will see that the sample used in **SURVEY** has a slight sex bias: Females are somewhat overrepresented in the sample relative to their percentage in the general population.)

Again the available options are listed in the menu across the bottom of the screen. *Press* the **down arrow** key. A slice has now been "exploded," and the information on that particular slice is shown at the lower right. We can now see that 42.7 percent of the sample is male. *Press* the **down arrow** again. The sample is 57.3 percent female.

On the legend to the left of the screen, you can see that the category "male" has a "0" in front of it and the category "female" has a "1" in front of it. Computers are more efficient working with numbers than with words, so researchers typically assign a number code to each category. For the present, simply ignore these number codes and focus on the category labels.

To see additional information on this variable, *type* **T** (for Table).

```
1) SEX
RESPONDENT'S SEX

Mean:          0.57      Std. Dev.:    0.49
Median:        0.63      N:            1,606      Missing:    0
99% confidence interval - mean:        0.54 to 0.61
95% confidence interval - mean:        0.55 to 0.60

               Frequency     %        Cum. %        Z-Score
MALE           685          42.7       42.7         -1.16
FEMALE         921          57.3      100.0          0.86
```

For now, ignore the information at the top of the screen and focus on the lower portion of the text. There were 685 males, or 42.7 percent of the sample, and 921 females, or 57.3 percent. Of course, the sum of the percentages must always add to 100. (In some cases, the actual sum may be very slightly larger or smaller due to rounding errors.) *Press* **B** (for Bar) to see the information presented in a bar graph. Figure 1.7 shows this graph (numbers on the vertical scale do not appear on the screen). Information on the bar above the arrow is shown at the lower left portion of the screen, so again we can see that 685 cases, or 42.7 percent, are males. *Press* the **right arrow**. The arrow moves the next bar, and the information at the lower left now applies to that bar, the females in the sample. *Press* *<ENTER>* to return to the beginning of the task.

Figure 1.7   Bar graph of 1) SEX

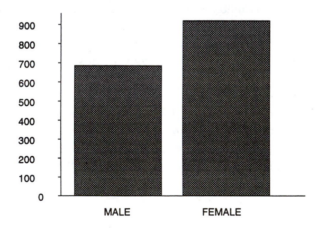

Press the **F3** key. If you look at the window at the lower right, you'll see that there are other uses for this window. The **A** key will put the list of variable names in alphabetic order. The **G** key will let you type the number of any variable you wish, and the highlight will shift to it. The **S** key will let you search the names and the descriptions of all variables for a key word; this search feature is a particularly useful way of finding variables dealing with particular topics.

Let's see if we can find any variable that deals with hunting. *Press* **S** (for Search). You are asked for a phrase. *Type* **HUNT** and *press* <ENTER>. Another window opens; this is the list of all variables that contain the letters "hunt" in their name or description. There is only one variable in this new window. *Press* the **right arrow** key. The respondents were asked if they had hunted or fished during the previous 12 months. *Press* <ENTER> to close the description window, and then *press* the **left arrow** key to select the variable. *Press* <ENTER> *twice* to close both windows. *Press* <ENTER> once again when asked about a subset. When the pie chart appears, *press* **D** (for Distribution). You can see that 560, or 35.2 percent, indicated that they had been hunting or fishing within the 12 months before the interview. *Press* **T** (for Table). You can also see that the N (number of cases) for the distribution is 1,591 and that 15 cases are missing. These cases failed to answer the question. The percentages shown are based on the number of cases who answered the question (1,591), not the number of cases in the sample (1,606). Some questions in the **SURVEY** data file were asked of only part of the sample (randomly selected). On those variables, many cases will have missing data.

Your turn.

1. *Open* the **USA** data file. Use the **F3** function key to find the description of each of the following variables:

   16) % RURAL
   Description:

   _____

   _____

   25) COUPLES
   Description:

   _____

   _____

   80) FOODSTAMPS
   Description:

   _____

   _____

2. *Select* the **Mapping** task.

   a. Map **72) HUNTING**. Record the values for the following states:

	RATE
IDAHO	_____
CALIFORNIA	_____
TEXAS	_____

   b. Map **109) MURDER**. Record the values for the following states:

	RATE
IDAHO	_____
CALIFORNIA	_____
TEXAS	_____

3. Map **71) FLD&STREAM**. What is the description of this variable?

_____

_____

   a. Record the values for the following states:

	RATE
IDAHO	_____
CALIFORNIA	_____
TEXAS	_____

   b. What are the three highest states and their rates?

	NAME	RATE
FIRST	_____	_____
SECOND	_____	_____
THIRD	_____	_____

   c. What are the three lowest states and their rates? (Omit states with missing data, if any.)

	NAME	RATE
THIRD LOWEST	_____	_____
SECOND LOWEST	_____	_____
LOWEST	_____	_____

   d. Compare the map of **71) FLD&STREAM** with each of the following and indicate if it is somewhat similar, opposite, or neither. Circle the correct answer.

72) HUNTING	Similar	Opposite	Neither
109) MURDER	Similar	Opposite	Neither
101) %NO RELIG.	Similar	Opposite	Neither

   e. Do you think there might be a connection between **71) FLD&STREAM** and the hunting license rate? Why or why not?

4. Map **56) SHRINKS**.

   a. What are the three states with the highest psychiatrist rates?

	NAME	RATE
FIRST	_____	_____
SECOND	_____	_____
THIRD	_____	_____

   b. What are the three states with the lowest psychiatrist rates? (Omit states with missing data.)

	NAME	RATE
THIRD LOWEST	_____	_____
SECOND LOWEST	_____	_____
LOWEST	_____	_____

   c. Compare this map of **56) SHRINKS** with each of the following and indicate if it is somewhat similar, opposite, or neither. Circle the correct answer.

67) GOURMET	Similar	Opposite	Neither
74) VETERANS	Similar	Opposite	Neither
82) HOME VALUE	Similar	Opposite	Neither
71) FLD&STREAM	Similar	Opposite	Neither

5. Map **105) CHURCH MEM**. *Press* **P** to print this map. (NOTE: If your computer is not connected to a printer or if you have been instructed not to use the printer, just skip these printing instructions.) When you print a graphic (e.g., a map or a bar graph), the program will ask whether you are using a laser or a dot matrix printer. Make the appropriate choice and *press* *<ENTER>*. (By the way, you need to specify the printer only once during any MicroCase session.) MicroCase will now print a copy of this map. (It may take some time—depending on the printer you are using—to print a graphic such as this.) Note that your name and the date will be printed along with the map.

   a. What is the description of this variable?

   _____

   _____

b. What are the three highest states?

	NAME	RATE
FIRST	_____	_____
SECOND	_____	_____
THIRD	_____	_____

c. What are the three lowest states? (Omit states with missing data.)

	NAME	RATE
THIRD LOWEST	_____	_____
SECOND LOWEST	_____	_____
LOWEST	_____	_____

d. Compare this map of **105) CHURCH MEM** with the **101) %NO RELIG.** map. Are they similar, opposite, or neither? (Circle one.)   Similar   Opposite   Neither

e. Does this make sense? Why or why not?

6. *Open* the **SURVEY** data file. Use the **F3** key to obtain the description and category labels for each of the following variables:

a. **37) POL.PARTY**

Description:

_____

_____

List the category labels:

1._____

2._____

3._____

b. **45) RELIGION**

Description:

_____

_____

List the category labels:

1._____

2._____

3._____

4._____

5._____

c. **15) DEGREE**

Description:

_____

_____

List the category labels:

1._____

2._____

3._____

7. Use the search function on the **F3** key to find variables using each of the following phrases:

a. INCOME
List the number and name of each variable:

b. HEALTH
   List the number and name of each variable:

c. MOTHER
   List the number and name of each variable:

8. *Select* the **Univariate** task. For each of the following variables, fill in the category labels, the frequency in each category, and the percent in each category.

	CATEGORY LABELS	FREQUENCY	%
a. **9) URBAN?**	_____	_____	_____
	_____	_____	_____
b. **45) RELIGION**	_____	_____	_____
	_____	_____	_____
	_____	_____	_____
	_____	_____	_____
	_____	_____	_____
c. **111) VISIT ART**	_____	_____	_____
	_____	_____	_____

That's all for this exercise. If you are not going to continue with the next exercise, it is very important to remember to exit properly from MicroCase by returning to one of the main menus and pressing the letter **X**.

1

Concepts and Theories

OVERVIEW

In this exercise, you will learn more about how we use concepts and theories in social research. The exercise also emphasizes the ability to recognize tautologies and the ability to identify testable statements. In addition you will learn to recognize normative statements based on values.

BEFORE YOU BEGIN

Please make sure that you have read Chapter 1 in the textbook and can answer the following review questions (you need not write any answers):

1. How are concepts and theories related to one another?

2. What is the difference between description and explanation?

3. What principles guide the construction of good concepts in social research?

4. What is a tautology?

5. What are the two essential features of theories in science?

6. Can theories be proven? Why or why not?

7. In relation to concepts, what are indicators?

8. How is the test of a hypothesis used to assess a theory?

9. What is the difference between induction and deduction?

10. What are empirical generalizations and how do they relate to induction?

11. What does it mean to say that there is a correlation between two variables?

Theoretical concepts do not stand alone, but rather are embedded in a set of relationships with other concepts. Concepts with the same name may have quite different meanings in different theories. Let's look at an example.

Sociologists have long been interested in social class, yet this concept means quite different things to different people. The Marxist perspective defines social class as the relationship of the individual to the means of production. Within this framework, there are two classes: those who own the means of production and those who don't. Other theoretical approaches divide societies into a greater number of classes, each of which can be distinguished clearly from the others.

Still other sociologists prefer to use the term *social status* since they see social status as a continuum rather than a set of identifiable classes. Even those who see social class as a continuum disagree on how it should be operationalized. Some see social class as a property of the individual, while others define it as a property of the individual's occupation. If social status, or class, is a property of the individual, then two individuals with the same occupation might have different social status. If social status is a function of the individual's occupation, then individuals with quite different incomes and educational levels but the same occupation will have the same social status.

None of these is the *true* definition of social class, and each definition suggests different empirical definitions. These definitions (and theories) will, however, differ in how useful they are in explaining the empirical world.

A concept should not be confused with a theory. For example, William Sims Bainbridge (1978)[1] observed an interesting phenomenon in his field study of Satan's Power, a satanic cult. When the cult first formed, members had friends outside the group as well as inside the group. As time passed, their social contacts outside the group began to decrease. This happened not only because some of the friends became members of the group, but also because members tended to stop seeing friends who were outside the cult. Eventually, members of the group had no contacts outside the group at all. Bainbridge called this phenomenon social implosion to describe how social relationships collapsed in upon themselves. However, naming this phenomenon added nothing to our understanding. We still don't know if this event was unique to this group or, if not, under what conditions members of groups tend to break off outside contacts or even what types of groups are likely to experience social implosion. Interesting as this phenomenon may be, we simply have a concept in need of a theory.

Confusing a concept with a theory is a relatively common problem. The difference between the two is that a theory is testable, or falsifiable, while a concept is not. We cannot say that social implosion caused this group to cut off outside contacts. Such a statement would be a tautology: Social implosion causes social

---

[1] Bainbridge, William Sims. 1978. *Satan's Power.* Berkeley: University of California Press.

implosion. On the other hand, the statement "The greater the punishment for nonconformity to group norms, the greater the likelihood that members of the group will cease contacts with outsiders" is, in principle, testable. "The more deviant the norms of the group from the norms of society, the more likely that members of the group will cease contacts with outsiders" is similarly, in principle, testable. The "in principle" caution means that we may encounter practical problems if we attempt to test the idea. For example, we may not be able to find enough appropriate groups, we may not be able to adequately measure the concept, we may encounter ethical problems, and so on.

Let's consider a second, more complicated example. Robert K. Merton (1938) created the following table:

		Uses Socially Approved Means	
		Yes	No
Seeks Socially Approved Goals	Yes	Conformist	Innovator
	No	Ritualist	Retreatist

This may appear to be a theory because two different concepts are involved, socially approved means and socially approved goals. However, all we have are four different definitions. A conformist, for example, is defined as one who seeks socially approved goals and uses socially approved means—anyone else is not a conformist. An innovator is defined as one who uses means that are not socially approved to seek socially approved goals—if this is not true of the individual, then the individual is not an innovator. Each of the two remaining types are defined in a similar manner. This is called a *typology* because a combination of two characteristics is used to define a set of types.

Assuming we have information on the means used and the goals desired by a particular individual, we can place him or her in the appropriate category or type. The statement "John Dillinger was an innovator *because* he used means that were not socially approved (robbing banks) to seek goals that were socially approved (money)" is a *tautology*—it is merely the application of the definition of innovator to John Dillinger. It is not a testable statement.

If this typology were linked to some other concept, then it would be more than a set of definitions. For example, the statement "Innovators will be more common under democracies than under other forms of government" and the statement "Innovators are more likely to obtain material rewards than are conformists" are both, in principle, testable.

Now, let's take a look at a theory and how it might be tested. Most theories of crime have focused on the criminal and the characteristics that lead individuals into a life of crime. Lawrence Cohen and Marcus Felson developed an approach to deviance called opportunity theory. They realized that having individuals with a propensity to commit crime may be necessary but is not sufficient for a crime to occur. There also needs to be an opportunity—without banks, there can be no bank robbers. A crime requires not only a person motivated to commit the offense, but also the presence of a suitable target (property or individual victims) and the absence of effective guardians. For example, this theory would predict that burglaries of homes will be more likely to occur during the daytime when everyone is at school or work (the absence of effective guardians) than in the evening when homes are occupied (the presence of effective guardians).

This is a testable statement. We can check the empirical truth or falsity of this statement. If it is false, we should reject the theory.[2] If it is true, then we can have greater faith in the theory. We can then conduct additional tests of this theory. Some empirical hypotheses provide stronger tests of theories than do others. In general, the riskier the prediction, the stronger the test. Suppose, for example, that the empirical prediction is well known to be true in advance of any research. Since we expect a theory to be consistent with known facts, this would not be a very strong test of the theory. However, if the empirical hypothesis is the opposite of what most social scientists would expect, then this would be a much stronger test of the theory.

Often a researcher may find support for a particular hypothesis and read into this additional, scientifically unjustified, conclusions. Consider a researcher who confirms the hypothesis that children who are spanked model the behavior of their parents and consequently engage in interpersonal violence. Beyond reporting this finding, the researcher adds that this study therefore proves that children should not be spanked. This is a *normative* conclusion, a statement that prescribes how people should behave based on some underlying set of values. That is, the conclusion does not logically follow from the assumptions but requires an additional value statement: Interpersonal violence is bad. Groups who value aggressive behavior might reach exactly the opposite conclusion. Normative statements cannot be evaluated in terms of true or false but only in terms of right or wrong and thus are not testable.

---

[2] In some cases, rather than reject the theory, we might reject the empirical evidence as an inadequate test of the theory. In this example, if a neighborhood has hired a security force to patrol during the daytime, then the theory would not predict a higher burglary rate during the day.

1. We have mentioned several different ways in which social class has been conceptualized. Select two different conceptualizations of social class and discuss how the difference between them would affect the indicators of social class used in research. (Attach an additional sheet if you need more space for your answer.)

2. *Civil religion* is the name applied to the use of religious symbols and rhetoric for public purposes and functions, especially political functions. *Civil religion* prompts U.S. presidents to mention God in their inaugural speeches. This also is the reason those in charge of designing U.S. money place "In God We Trust" on coins.

    Based on materials in the textbook and the earlier discussion in this exercise, evaluate the last two sentences in the above paragraph. Does civil religion explain why U.S. presidents mention God and why "In God We Trust" is placed on coins? Discuss your answer.

3. The famous German sociologist Max Weber (1864–1920) introduced the concept of charisma to describe the situation where a leader's power is believed to rest upon divine authority—that the leader has a divine right to rule. The word itself is Greek and means "divine gift." Social scientists frequently attribute charisma to leaders. For example, because the Pope has so much charisma, many people accept his divine right to lead Christianity.

    Evaluate the last sentence in this paragraph.

4. For each of the following statements, circle **T** if the statement is, in principle, testable or **NT** if the statement is not testable. Then, since the testability of a statement may depend on how you interpret certain elements, explain your answer in one sentence.

a. New York state has a lower murder rate than the state of North Dakota.　　　　　　　　　　　　　　T　　NT

b. The United States should prohibit capital punishment.　　　T　　NT

c. Persons who are anti-Semitic hate Jews.　　　　　　　　　T　　NT

d. The moon is made of blue cheese.　　　　　　　　　　　　T　　NT

e. Individuals should not be allowed to own assault rifles.　　T　　NT

f. Citizens have greater political freedom in France than in Japan.　　　　　　　　　　　　　　　　　　T　　NT

5. For each of the following statements, circle **Yes** if the statement is a tautology or **No** if the statement is not a tautology.

    a. Jim is not married because he is a bachelor.   Yes   No

    b. Illinois has a lower crime rate than California
       because Illinois is less urban than California.   Yes   No

    c. Becky Sue has low self-esteem because nobody
       likes her.   Yes   No

    d. Clancy votes Democratic because he belongs to
       the union.   Yes   No

    e. Karen works in a fast-food restaurant because
       she needs the money.   Yes   No

    f. Arson is a crime because it is against the law.   Yes   No

    g. Bob is in prison because he was convicted of murder. Yes   No

    h. Dick is a felon because he was convicted of murder. Yes   No

    i. You won't be popular if not enough people like you. Yes   No

    j. Anyone can win an election if he or she gets
       enough votes.   Yes   No

6. a. Give three additional empirical predictions from the opportunity theory of crime developed by Cohen and Felson.

       1.

       2.

       3.

b. Assuming you have great confidence in this theory, how could you apply the ideas to crime prevention programs?

7. In Appendix B, look at the **SURVEY** codebook information for variables **42) HELP HUSB**, **43) HOUSEWIFE**, and **44) MEN BETTER**. Note that these questions are based on normative statements and that we cannot prove or disprove these statements scientifically. However, in social research we often study the views that people hold on such matters. Find two other variables in the **SURVEY** file that are based on normative statements and list them below.

a. Number:_____   Name:_____
   Description:

   _____

   _____

b. Number:_____   Name:_____
   Description:

   _____

   _____

2a

The Research Process Using Aggregate Data

OVERVIEW

In this exercise, you will learn more about the stages of the social research process and you will experience some of these stages directly. Specifically, you will gain experience in formulating hypotheses, selecting indicators to operationalize concepts, and using statistical results to test hypotheses. You will also see differences in the ways we utilize two different kinds of data: aggregate data and survey data.

BEFORE YOU BEGIN

Please make sure you have read Chapter 2 in the textbook and can answer the following review questions (you need not write any answers):

1. What are the general stages in the research process?

2. What does *operationalize a concept* mean and how are *indicators* used in this process?

3. What is replication research and why is it important?

Many of us are concerned about violent crimes, and we wonder why some people are more likely than others to commit such crimes. Learning theorists would argue that violent criminal activities are learned in the same way that other behaviors are learned. According to this approach, to understand violent behavior, we need to see how the behavior is learned. This has led some social scientists to speculate that there should be a connection between hunting and violent crime: Hunting encourages the learning of violent behaviors, and, once learned, they can be applied to humans as well as to animals.

At this point, we have completed two steps in the research process: **select our topic** (Step 1) and **formulate our research question** (Step 2). The research question is simply, "Is there a connection between hunting and violent behavior?" Next we need to **define the concepts** (Step 3):

> Hunting: the pursuit and killing of wild, game animals for sport or for food
>
> Violent behavior: physical violence, or threat of physical violence, toward another individual

Both of these concepts apply only to behaviors outside of a regular occupational role. Killing animals in an occupational role—what meat packers, chicken farmers, and humane society workers do—is not considered hunting. Further, let's exclude the threat of violence by a police officer or in a military setting from our definition of violent behavior.

When we define concepts, we also introduce the possibility that others will disagree with the definition. Because we are interested in hunting behavior, not in its motivation, we have included both hunting for food and hunting for sport in our definition. If we were testing other ideas concerned with motivation for hunting, our definition might exclude hunting for food.

We now need to **operationalize our concepts** (Step 4)—to select the indicators of these concepts. In this exercise, we'll use the **USA** data file to test this idea.

Start MicroCase using the instructions in the *Getting Started* section of the Introduction. With the highlight on **I. Open, Look, Erase or Copy File**, *press <ENTER>*. The available data files are now listed. Using the **arrow** keys, place the highlight on **USA** and *press <ENTER>*. This data set is based on aggregates, rather than individuals: each case, or state, is a collection, or aggregation, of individuals.

We already know that we have information on hunting licenses in this data file. This could be used as our indicator of the extent of hunting in each state. *Press* the F3 key and *press* the **right arrow**. Scroll through the variable descriptions and see if you can find a variable that could be used as an indicator of violent behavior across the states.

Let's use variable 109) MURDER as our indicator of violent behavior. If the idea that hunting affects violent behavior is true, then we would expect states to be relatively high on both variables or to be relatively low on both variables. In other words, we would expect the maps of the two variables to look alike. We can now **formulate our hypothesis** (Step 5): States with high rates of hunting licenses will tend to have high murder rates. We are now ready to make the observations.

We are fortunate that the appropriate observations have already been collected and are included in the **USA** data set, so we can skip step 6, **make the observations,** and move directly to **analyze the data** (Step 7).

Go to the **STATISTICAL ANALYSIS** menu and map **72** or **HUNTING**. (There is a *Quick Guide for MicroCase* on the inside front cover in case you need it.) *Press* **C** (for Compare). This task will allow us to look at two maps on the same screen. The map of hunting licenses is redrawn at the top of the screen, and we may now select a second map. *Type* **109** and *press* <ENTER>. The map of 109) MURDER is now drawn in the lower half of the screen. See Figure 2.1.

The maps don't look at all alike; in fact, they appear to be almost opposites. Based on visual inspection, we would conclude that the two rates don't vary together. We have now finished Step 8—**assess the results**. (If this were an actual study, we would still have two steps remaining: publish the findings and replicate the research.)

Figure 2.1   Comparison of 72) HUNTING and 109) MURDER

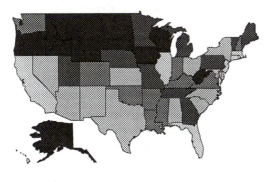

1990: NUMBER OF
RESIDENTS WHO
PURCHASED HUNTING
LICENSES PER 1,000
POPULATION
(U.S. FISH & WILDLIFE)

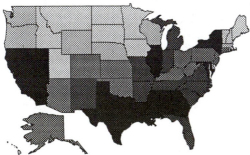

1992: HOMICIDES
PER 100,000
POPULATION (UCR)

Press <ENTER>, type **71**, *and press <ENTER> again.* As shown in Figure 2.2, these two maps look very much alike. However, conclusions from simply inspecting maps can be fairly subjective; our personal opinions may influence how we view the maps. So it is preferable to be able to quantify how alike or how different two maps are.

Figure 2.2   Comparison of 72) HUNTING and 71) FLD&STREAM

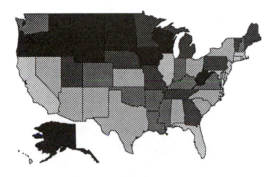

1990: NUMBER OF
RESIDENTS WHO
PURCHASED HUNTING
LICENSES PER 1,000
POPULATION (U.S. FISH &
WILDLIFE)

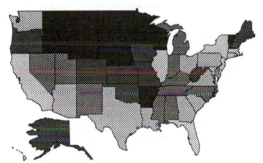

1990: CIRCULATION OF
FIELD & STREAM
MAGAZINE PER
100,000 POPULATION
(ABC)

Fortunately, there is a statistical technique that will allow us to do this. *Press <ENTER>* as many times as necessary to return to the **STATISTICAL ANALYSIS** menu. (Or you can *press* the **<ESC>** key and answer **Y** to the prompt to return to the main menu.) *Select* **F. Scatterplot** from the menu. *Select* **71** or **FLD&STREAM** (the circulation of *Field and Stream* magazine per 100,000 population) as the dependent variable and *select* **72** or **HUNTING** (the number of hunting licenses per 1,000 population) as the independent variable. *Press <ENTER>* to skip the selection of a subset. A graphic appears in the middle of the screen. See Figure 2.3.

The y-axis is the line at the left labeled FLD&STREAM; the values on this axis range from 338 to 2009. This vertical axis represents all values of 71) FLD&STREAM that we saw earlier on the map. The x-axis is the line at the bottom of the graph labeled HUNTING; the values on this axis range from 11.7 to

586.4. This horizontal axis represents all values of 72) HUNTING that we also displayed earlier in a map.

Figure 2.3   Scatterplot between 71) FLD&STREAM and 72) HUNTING

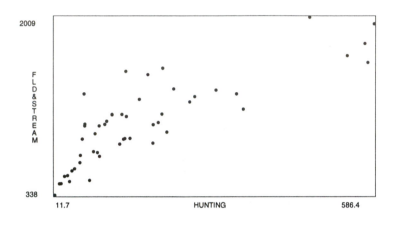

Each dot on the graph represents a state and its values on these two variables. Let's see how this works. In the first exercise, you recorded the values of three states on each of these variables. Idaho had a value of 1947 on 71) FLD&STREAM, so it would be close to the top on the y-axis. In your mind, draw a horizontal line at approximately 1947 on the y-axis. Idaho has a value of 586.4 on 72) HUNTING, so it would be at the far right of the x-axis. Mentally draw a vertical line at the far right of the graph. The intersection of these two lines represents Idaho.

Press **S** (for Show case). *Type* **IDAHO** and *press* <ENTER>. (You don't need to type the whole name, just enough letters to uniquely identify it—ID would be enough.) A dot at the upper right of the screen will start flashing. This dot is located where the two lines would intersect and represents Idaho on both variables. The value of Idaho on each variable (listed as X and Y) is shown in the lower right of the screen. *Press* <ENTER> and the dot will stop flashing. You might want to find the location of some other states. When you have finished, *press* <ENTER> to return to the scatterplot.

Press **L** (for regression Line). A line now appears on the graph, as shown in Figure 2.4. This line represents the best effort to draw a *straight* line that connects all of the dots. It is unnecessary for you to know how to calculate the location of the regression line—the program does it for you. But if you would like to see how the regression line would look if the maps were identical, all you need to do is examine the scatterplot using the same variable for both the x-axis and the y-axis. All the dots would be on the line.

Figure 2.4   Scatterplot between 71) FLD&STREAM and 72) HUNTING with regression line

In the current example, the maps are similar but not identical, so the dots are scattered near, but not on, the regression line. Now we need a method of determining how close these dots are to the line. *Press* **R** (for Residual). See Figure 2.5. A vertical line now connects each dot to the line; if we sum these distances, we can get a measure of how much alike the two maps are. The smaller this sum, the more alike are the two maps, or variables. For example, when the maps are identical and all the dots are on the regression line, the sum of these distances is zero.

Figure 2.5   Scatterplot between 71) FLD&STREAM and 72) HUNTING with residuals

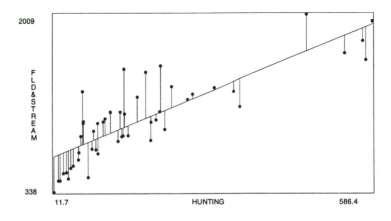

This idea is used to calculate the value of a statistic called the *correlation coefficient*. The value of this coefficient can vary from –1 to +1. When the value is 1, the two maps are identical; when the value is –1, they are opposites. When the value is zero, they are neither similar nor opposites. *Press <ENTER> to return to the scatterplot.* At the bottom of the scatterplot, we can see that the correlation (indicated using a lowercase r) between hunting licenses and circulation of *Field and Stream* magazine is .829. This shows a very strong relationship between these two variables.

When the value of the correlation coefficient gets close to zero, we may worry that the relationship was simply created by chance factors, such as inaccurate measurements. How large must a correlation be to indicate that a relationship between the two variables actually exists? Using probability theory, statisticians can tell us how likely we are to observe a particular correlation coefficient by chance when there is really no relationship. (Do you see the prob. = 0.000 result shown on the screen?) If this probability is small enough, then we can reject the hypothesis of no relationship, supporting the hypothesis that there is a relationship. In social science, the level of .05 is used for this rejection point—that is, if this correlation coefficient would be observed less than 5 times in 100 when there is no relationship, then we will conclude that a relationship probably exists. This is called the *statistical significance level*. Some researchers are even more stringent and use .01 as the rejection point. (In Chapter 4, these issues will be discussed in greater deal.)

Let's go back to our research hypothesis about hunting and murder and look at the scatterplot for those two variables. *Press <ENTER> to return to the beginning of the task. Select* **109** or **MURDER** as the dependent variable and *select* **72** or **HUNTING** as the independent variable. *Press <ENTER> to skip the subset option.* After the map appears, *press* **L** (for regression Line). As you can see in Figure 2.6, the regression line slopes *downward* and the correlation (–0.466) between these two variables is negative and quite strong. This relationship is significant at the .05 level (prob. = 0.000).

This means that the empirical data actually go in the opposite direction from that predicted—the higher the hunting license rate, the lower the murder rate! At this point, we would want to assess whether we really have provided a test of our research question. Perhaps we did not properly operationalize the concepts. Perhaps the observations are incorrect. There are other such problems that could have influenced the results. Some empirical observations provide much stronger tests of hypotheses than do others. By the end of the course, you should understand why this was not a particularly strong test.

Figure 2.6:   Scatterplot between 109) MURDER and 72) HUNTING

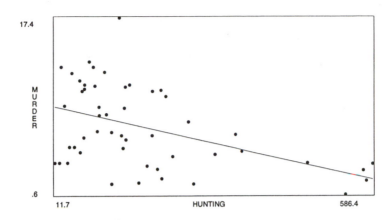

However, for the present, let's assume that this was a strong test of a theory and that the empirical hypothesis was, in fact, a proper application of the theory. What can we conclude about the theory? Finding that the empirical hypothesis was false should lead us to reject the theory from which it was derived. The implications of the theory were wrong, therefore the theory itself must be false. On the other hand, if the empirical hypothesis were true, we could not conclude that the theory is *true*. We might have more faith in the theory, but we could not *prove* the theory. (You might want to reread the discussion of the relationship between theory and empirical observations in Chapter 1 of the text to understand this better.)

In the present example, you might find it tempting to decide that we should have used another theoretical approach. For example, you might suggest that hunting is a substitute form of violence and individuals who hunt have no need for other outlets for violent behavior. Creative social scientists could probably come up with many different ideas that would be consistent with this empirical result. However, we can't claim to have tested any of these alternatives, because we constructed them after we already knew the results of the test. Explanations of this type are called *ex post facto*—created after the fact. For research to be a valid test of a theory, the empirical hypothesis must be derived from the theory before the relevant analysis is conducted.

Incidentally, findings that fail to support a hypothesis are also important. In fact, a strong test that raises serious questions about an existing theory may change the whole course of a scientific field. Sometimes taking a step backward is really a leap forward.

The scatterplot technique we have just used is the basis for the first correlation coefficient (developed by Karl Pearson in the 1890s), and there are many variant methods based on the same underlying logic. However, it is not necessary to actually create a scatterplot in order to calculate r (the correlation coefficient), and thus it is possible to calculate many correlations at the same time.

Press <ENTER> until you have returned to the **STATISTICAL ANALYSIS** menu. Place the highlight on **G. Correlation** and *press <ENTER>*. When the screen asks for the name or number of variable 1, *select* **109** or **MURDER**. The screen will ask for the name or number of variable 2. *Select* **72** or **HUNTING**. *Select* **73** or **FISHING** for the third variable and **70** or **PICKUPS** for variable 4. *Press <ENTER> twice* and this screen will appear:

	109)MURDER	72)HUNTING	73)FISHING	70)PICKUPS
109)MURDER	1.000	-0.466**	-0.256*	-0.190
72)HUNTING	-0.466**	1.000	0.773**	0.709**
73)FISHING	-0.256*	0.773**	1.000	0.609**
70)PICKUPS	-0.190	0.709**	0.609**	1.000

What you are looking at is called a *correlation matrix*. In it you can see the correlations between each pair of the four variables. Looking at the far left, we see that there is a perfect correlation (1.000) between 109) MURDER and 109) MURDER, as there should be since these are the same measures. Looking down the diagonal from left to right, we can see that in fact each variable is perfectly correlated with itself. Reading down the far left column, we can see the correlation between the murder rate and each of the other three variables. The correlation with 72) HUNTING is the same as we have seen with the scatterplot. The negative signs indicate that, as each of these rates rises, the murder rate declines. Two asterisks indicate that a correlation is significant beyond the .01 level, while one asterisk indicates significance beyond the .05 level. Notice that the correlation between 109) MURDER and 70) PICKUPS (the number of pickup trucks per 1,000 population) lacks an asterisk. That means it is not statistically significant and should be regarded as zero.

In addition to showing the correlation of each variable with 109) MURDER, the matrix shows the correlations between each pair of variables. To find the correlation between any two variables, first find the name of one variable across the top of the table and then find the name of the other down the left side. Locate the cell where the two variables coincide and that is the correlation coefficient between them. Thus, for example, the correlation between 72) HUNTING and 70) PICKUPS is 0.709**, and between 72) HUNTING and 73) FISHING it is 0.773**.

In addition to letting you use the scatterplot and correlation tasks for obtaining correlations, MicroCase lets you see the correlation between any two aggregate variables through the compare map function. Let's take a look at this. *Press <ENTER>* until you are back on the **STATISTICAL ANALYSIS** menu. Place the highlight on **E. Mapping Variables** and *press <ENTER>*. Map **109** or **MURDER**. *Press* **C** (for Compare). When the screen asks for the name or number of the variable for comparison, *select* **71** or **FLD&STREAM**. Your screen will look like Figure 2.7.

Figure 2.7   Comparison of 109) MURDER and 71) FLD&STREAM

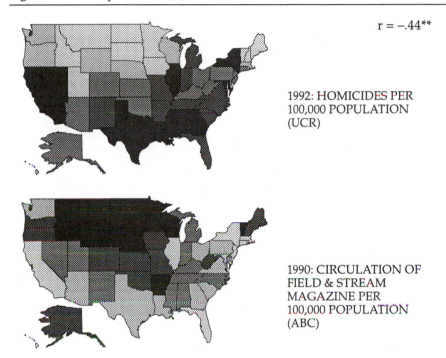

r = −.44**

1992: HOMICIDES PER
100,000 POPULATION
(UCR)

1990: CIRCULATION OF
FIELD & STREAM
MAGAZINE PER
100,000 POPULATION
(ABC)

Notice that the two maps tend to be reverse images, indicating a negative correlation. But instead of relying on visual comparisons of these two maps, look at the upper right-hand corner of the screen. See −.44**. That is the correlation coefficient between these two variables. Whenever you use the compare maps function, the correlation automatically appears.

Your turn.

NAME:

COURSE:

DATE:

EXERCISE

2a

Workbook exercises and software are copyrighted. Copying is prohibited by law.

WORKSHEET

1. a. If necessary, start MicroCase and *open* the **USA** data file. There are other ways in which we could have operationalized physical violence. Use the **F3** function key and scroll the variable descriptions. Find two other indicators of physical violence in the **USA** data file and write information about them below.

First indicator:
Number:_____   Name:_____
Description:

_____

_____

Second indicator:
Number:_____   Name:_____
Description:

_____

_____

b. Now, using the **Scatterplot** task, test the hypothesis that hunting is correlated with rates of physical violence using each of the above indicators. Construct your hypotheses *before* you look at the scatterplots.

Hypothesis 1: Hunting will be (circle choice) positively/negatively correlated with _____.
                                        (first indicator)

Using the **Scatterplot** task, *select* your first indicator as the dependent variable and **72** or **HUNTING** as the independent variable.

Value of r?   r = _____

Is relationship positive or negative? (Circle one.)   Positive   Negative

Level of significance?   Prob. = _____

Is this hypothesis supported? (Circle one.)   Yes   No

c. *Hypothesis 2:* Hunting will be (circle one) positively/negatively
correlated with _____.
                           (second indicator)

Using the **Scatterplot** task, *select* your second indicator as the dependent
variable and **72** or **HUNTING** as the independent variable.

Value of r?   r = _____

Is relationship positive or negative? (Circle one.)   Positive   Negative

Level of significance?   Prob. = _____

Is this hypothesis supported? (Circle one.)   Yes   No

2.   As explained in Chapter 1 of the text, evaluation research often is not
     prompted by theory testing but tests empirical claims that some program or
     policy had its intended effect. To explore an example of such research, let's
     test this hypothesis: Drug education programs will reduce the incidence of
     drug abuse. To do so, create the following scatterplot:

                   Dependent variable: **44) COKE USERS**
                   Independent variable: **45) DRUG ED**

a. Write in the description for **44) COKE USERS** (*press* **Y** to see it; then *press*
   <ENTER> to close the window).

   _____

   _____

b. Write in the description for **45) DRUG ED** (*press* **X** to see it).

   _____

   _____

c. What is the correlation coefficient?   r = _____

d. Is the correlation positive or negative?
   (Circle one.)   Positive   Negative

e. Level of significance?   Prob. = _____

f. Is this hypothesis supported or rejected? (Circle one.)   Support   Reject

g. Assuming this were the only evidence available, what conclusion would you draw about the effectiveness of drug education programs?

3. Next, test this hypothesis: School dropout rates can be reduced by increased spending on education. To do so, create the following scatterplot:

   Dependent variable: **91) DROPOUTS**
   Independent variable: **93) $PER PUPIL**

a. Write in the description for **91) DROPOUTS** (*press* **Y** to see it).

_____

_____

b. Write in the description for **93 or $PER PUPIL** (*press* **X** to see it).

_____

_____

c. What is the correlation coefficient?   r = _____

d. Is the correlation positive or negative?
   (Circle one.)   Positive   Negative

e. Level of significance?   Prob. = _____

f. Is this hypothesis supported or rejected?
   (Circle one.)   Support   Reject

g. Assuming this were the only evidence available, what conclusion would you draw about the effectiveness of increased school spending programs?

4. Sometimes researchers do exploratory studies. They develop an interest in
    some phenomenon, but don't understand it well enough to formulate
    hypotheses. So they poke around and try this or that, in order to gain suffi-
    cient understanding to permit them to formulate hypotheses. Suppose you
    became interested in wine consumption rates and wanted to get some idea
    of the social contexts in which wine is more popular compared with other
    forms of alcoholic beverages.

    The best way to start is simply to map **47** or **% WINE**. When the map is on the
    screen, *press* **S** (for Spot) to gain a clearer picture of where a higher percentage
    of alcohol is sold in the form of wine. *Press* **D** (for Distribution) and see the 50
    states ranked from highest to lowest. Fill in the information requested next:

    The 8 highest states are: The 8 lowest states are:

    1._____   43._____

    2._____   44._____

    3._____   45._____

    4._____   46._____

    5._____   47._____

    6._____   48._____

    7._____   49._____

    8._____   50._____

    Looking both at the map and at these lists, in what region or regions is wine
    most popular?_____

    Press **P** to print this distribution. (NOTE: If your computer is not connected
    to a printer or if you have been instructed not to use the printer, just skip
    these printing instructions.)

    a. Now, return to the map and *press* **C** (for Compare). The map of wine con-
        sumption will move to the top of the screen, and the screen will ask for
        the name or number of the variable to be compared. Use **67** or
        GOURMET.

        Write in the caption for the second map: _____

        _____

        What is the correlation coefficient?   r = _____

        Is the correlation positive or negative? (Circle one.)   Positive   Negative

b. *Press <ENTER>* to compare a new map. Use **65** or **ARC.DIGEST**.

Write in the caption for the second map: _____

_____

What is the correlation coefficient? r = _____

Is the correlation positive or negative? (Circle one.)   Positive   Negative

c. *Press <ENTER>* to compare a new map. Use **90** or **% COLLEGE**.

Write in the caption for the second map: _____

_____

What is the correlation coefficient? r = _____

Is the correlation positive or negative? (Circle one.)   Positive   Negative

d. *Press <ENTER>* to compare a new map. Use **17** or **% METROPOL**.

Write in the caption for the second map: _____

_____

What is the correlation coefficient? r = _____

Is the correlation positive or negative? (Circle one.)   Positive   Negative

e. *Press <ENTER>* to compare a new map. Use **51** or **% FAT**.

Write in the caption for the second map: _____

_____

What is the correlation coefficient? r = _____

Is the correlation positive or negative? (Circle one.)   Positive   Negative

f. *Press <ENTER>* to compare a new map. Use **16** or **% RURAL**.

Write in the caption for the second map: _____

_____

What is the correlation coefficient? r = _____

Is the correlation positive or negative? (Circle one.)   Positive   Negative

g. *Press <ENTER>* to compare a new map. Use **71** or **FLD&STREAM**.

Write in the caption for the second map: _____

_____

What is the correlation coefficient?   r = _____

Is the correlation positive or negative? (Circle one.)   Positive   Negative

h. Based on these correlations, see if you can identify an underlying concept of which each of these variables may be an indicator. Define and explain this concept. Keep in mind that there is no single *right* answer—many somewhat similar concepts would be quite appropriate here. Keep in mind too that some indicators can be negative measures of a concept in the same sense that clean air can be a positive measure of the quality of life in cities while the violent crime rate can be a negative indicator of the quality of life.

i. Looking through the codebook, find two additional indicators that you expect to be positive indicators of the concept you have identified. Using the compare maps function, answer the following questions:

Name and number of the first additional indicator: _____

Correlation with **47) % WINE**:   r = _____

Is the correlation positive or negative? (Circle one.)   Positive   Negative

Name and number of the second additional indicator: _____

Correlation with **47) % WINE**:   r = _____

Is the correlation positive or negative? (Circle one.)   Positive   Negative

Do these results confirm their selection as positive
indicators of your concept? (Circle one.)   Yes   No

j. Looking through the codebook, find two additional indicators that you
   expect to be negative indicators of the concept you have identified. Using
   the compare maps function, answer the following questions:

   Name and number of the first additional indicator: _____

   Correlation with **47) % WINE**:   r = _____

   Is the correlation positive or negative? (Circle one.)   Positive   Negative

   Name and number of the second additional indicator: _____

   Correlation with **47) % WINE**:   r = _____

   Is the correlation positive or negative? (Circle one.)   Positive   Negative

   Do these results confirm their selection as negative
   indicators of your concept? (Circle one.)   Yes   No

k. If the president of a winery asked you to characterize the sorts of places
   where wine sells best, what would you say?

2b

The Research Process Using Survey Data

In the previous exercise, we worked through an example of the research process using the **USA** data set. Here we will examine how to study a different research question using data on individuals. In recent years, health care reform has been the subject of a heated debate. Many individuals would like the federal government to take a more active role in the administration of health care, while others prefer to leave health care in the private sector. There are many issues in this debate, but a basic disagreement is simply over the appropriate role of the federal government in programs of this type. In general, should government be more active or less active in the day-to-day life of citizens? Those with more liberal political views favor increasing the role of government, while conservatives favor limiting its role. We would expect this difference of opinion to extend to the area of health care. So we have our first research hypothesis: Those with conservative political views are less likely to favor government intervention in health care than are those with liberal political views.

We also might expect that those who are likely to be excluded under the current health care system would favor more participation by the government. We'll also test this second hypothesis.

Start MicroCase and *open* the **SURVEY** data file. Let's see if we can find some variables that can be used as indicators of the relevant concepts. *Press* the **F3** key. Place the highlight on **49** or **GOV.MED.** and *press* the **right arrow** key; this variable has the following description: 1) IT IS THE RESPONSIBILITY OF GOVERNMENT TO HELP 2) PEOPLE SHOULD TAKE CARE OF THEMSELVES. This could be used as an indicator of whether individuals favor government participation in health care.

Move the highlight to **36** or **POL.VIEW** and look at its description. This question could be used as an indicator of the individual's position on the liberal/conservative continuum. We also could use party preference, 37) POL.PARTY, and how the person voted in the 1992 presidential election, 39) WHO IN 92?, as other indicators of political conservatism.

To test the second hypothesis, we need to determine who is likely to be excluded under the current health care system. Paid health care is usually not included as a benefit for low-income jobs; so 23) INCOME might be used as an indicator of those excluded. Unemployed individuals are often uncovered as well, so 27) EVER UNEMP might be used as another indicator.

The data already have been collected so we can move to the analysis stage. Close the windows and continue to the menu. Move to the **STATISTICAL ANALYSIS** menu. First, let's look at the distribution of **49) GOV.MED.** *Select* **A. Univariate Statistics** and *select* **49** or **GOV.MED.** *Press* <ENTER> in response to the question about a subset. A pie chart will result, as shown in Figure 2.8. *Press* **D** (for Distribution). We can see that 51.8 percent of the sample agreed that the government should cover medical costs. *Press* **T** (for Table). We can see that there were 580 cases with missing data—they either were not asked the question or did not answer. Remember that missing data are excluded in all calculations, so the percentages are based on only those cases with data (1,026). *Press* <ENTER> *twice* to return to the **STATISTICAL ANALYSIS** menu.

Figure 2.8   Pie chart of 49) GOV.MED.

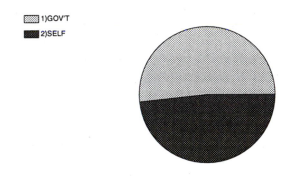

Select **B. Tabular Statistics.** *Select* **49** or **GOV.MED.** as the row variable and **36** or **POL. VIEW** as the column variable. *Press* <ENTER> when asked for a control variable and again to skip the subset option:

Row Variable: 49) GOV.MED.   Column Variable: 36) POL.VIEW

	LIBERAL	MODERATE	CONSERV.	Missing	TOTAL
GOV'T.	173	182	163	13	518
SELF	103	168	207	17	478
Missing	137	225	190	28	580
TOTAL	276	350	370	58	996

This table shows the distribution of attitude toward government participation in health care within each category of political views. For example, 173 cases indicated that they were liberal and that they supported government health care, 182 cases were moderate and supported government health care, and so on. As in the **Univariate Statistics** task, missing data are omitted from all calculations, so the total for the first *row* is 518 (173 + 182 + 163), and the total for the first *column* is 276 (173 + 103).

Looking at the table, we can see that, of the 276 liberals, 173 favored government health care and 103 did not. Looking at the next column, we can see that there were more moderates (182) than liberals who favored government health care but also more moderates (168) than liberals who did not. This is because there were more moderates (350) than liberals (276).

This makes it obvious that we can't simply compare raw numbers of respondents. We must take differences in the size of populations into account. To do so, we can calculate the percentage of the group in each category. Since we want to compare the views on health care across the liberal/conservative political spectrum, *press* **C** (for Column percentaging):

```
Row Variable: 49 GOV.MED.      Column Variable: 36 POL.VIEW
```

	LIBERAL	MODERATE	CONSERV.	Missing	TOTAL
GOV'T.	173	182	163	13	518
	62.7	52.0	44.1		52.0
SELF	103	168	207	17	478
	37.3	48.0	55.9		48.0
Missing	137	225	190	28	580
TOTAL	276	350	370	58	996
	100.0	100.0	100.0		100.0

Looking at the second row of numbers and reading from left to right, we now can see that 62.7 percent of the liberals favored government health care, 52.0 of the moderates did, and 44.1 percent of the conservatives did. So the differences are in the predicted direction. However, this table is based on a sample of the population, and a sample is extremely unlikely to be exactly like the population from which it is drawn. Can we be sure that this relationship actually exists in the population? *Press* **S** (for Statistics). Look at the section of the screen labeled *nominal statistics*:

```
Nominal Statistics
Chi-Square:      21.975      DF:             2          (Prob. = 0.000)
V:               0.149       C:              0.147
Lambda(DV=36):   0.030       Lambda(DV=49):  0.092      Lambda:    0.057
```

Chi-square is a statistic calculated from this table. Using probability theory, statisticians can tell us how likely we are to observe a particular chi-square value by chance when there is no relationship in the population. If this probability is small enough then we can reject the hypothesis of no relationship, supporting the hypothesis that there is a relationship. In this example, the probability (Prob. = 0.000) is extremely low. Consequently, we can be pretty sure that there really is a relationship between these two variables in the population. In social science, the level of .05 is used for this rejection point—if this value of chi-square would be observed less than 5 times in 100 when there is no relationship, then we will conclude that a relationship probably exists. This is called the *statistical significance level*. (In Chapter 4, these issues will be discussed in greater detail.)

We also can make use of another statistic on this screen, Cramer's V. The value of V tells us how strong the relationship is. This is analogous to Pearson's correlation coefficient (r) which we used when looking at scatterplots. V can range from 0 to 1. A value of 0 indicates no relationship between the two variables, and a value of 1 is the strongest possible relationship. In this example, V has a value of 0.149. There's one extremely important way in which V is different than Pearson's r. Pearson's r tells us how well a straight line fits the data and also the direction of the relationship. V tells us nothing about the nature of the relationship, only about its strength. We must look at the table itself to describe the relationship. For example, if the values in the liberal and conservative column had been swapped, the value of V would be exactly the same. However, the table (with the swapped columns) would show that conservatives are more likely to support government health care and would consequently fail to support our hypothesis. When examining a relationship using tabular analysis, you must interpret the actual table, as well as examine the value and significance of V.

Let's try another test of the first hypothesis. *Press <ENTER> twice* to return to the beginning of the task. *Select* **49** or **GOV.MED.** as the row variable and **37** or **POL.PARTY** as the column variable. Do not select a control variable and do not select a subset. *Press* **C** (for Column percentages). (For the rest of the workbook, only the percentages and the total number of cases for each column will be shown.)

Row Variable: 49) GOV.MED.   Column Variable: 37) POL.PARTY

	DEMOCRAT	INDEPENDENT	REPUBLICAN
GOV'T.	60.5	55.5	40.1
SELF	39.5	44.5	59.9
N	483	128	399

We see the same pattern here as well: Democrats are more likely than Independents and Independents are more likely than Republicans to endorse government health care. *Press* **S** (for Statistics). This is also statistically significant at less than the .05 level, and Cramer's V is .192.

Let's test our hypothesis yet another time. *Press <ENTER> twice* to return to the beginning of the task and use **49** or **GOV.MED.** as the row variable and **39** or **WHO IN 92?** as the column variable. Do not select a control variable and do not subset. When the table appears, make sure to use column percentages.

Row Variable: 49) GOV.MED.	Column Variable: 39) WHO IN 92?		
	CLINTON	BUSH	PEROT
GOV'T.	64.5	34.9	50.4
SELF	35.5	65.1	49.6
N	301	261	125

We can see that those who voted for Clinton were more likely to favor government health care than those who voted for Bush or for Perot. Those who voted for Perot were more likely to favor government health care than those who voted for Bush. *Press* **S** (for Statistics). This is also statistically significant at the .05 level, and V is .267. (Since our hypothesis really should be limited to the Democratic and Republican candidates, we should have used the subset feature to eliminate the Perot voters. We'll see how to use this feature later in the workbook.)

All three tests of the first research hypothesis provided support for it. Let's turn to our second hypothesis. Return to the beginning of the task and *select* **49** or **GOV.MED.** as the row variable and **23** or **INCOME** as the column variable. Do not select a control variable and do not subset. Use column percentaging:

Row Variable: 49) GOV.MED.	Column Variable: 23) INCOME		
	UNDER 15K	15K-29999K	30K & OVER
GOV'T.	56.2	56.2	48.6
SELF	43.8	43.8	51.4
N	226	226	486

There is no difference between those with family incomes under $15,000 and those with family incomes between $15,000 and $30,000. The difference between these two income groups and the highest income group is in the predicted direction, but the difference is not large. *Press* **S** (for Statistics). We can see the relationship is not statistically significant at the .05 level (Prob. = 0.065). So this fails to support our second hypothesis. Why?

It is possible that income is not a good indicator of those who have been excluded from the health care system. Medicare and Medicaid are already paying for at least some health care among the poor, especially the elderly poor. Let's try another test of this hypothesis. Return to the beginning of the task.

Select **49** or **GOV.MED.** as the row variable and **27** or **EVER UNEMP** (Have you ever been unemployed for as long as a month in the past 10 years?) as the column variable. Do not select a control variable or a subset. Look at the column percentages:

Row Variable: 49) GOV.MED.	Column Variable: 27) EVER UNEMP	
	YES	NO
GOV'T	60.1	48.0
OTHER	39.9	52.0
N	336	686

The results are in the predicted direction and the difference is fairly large. *Press* **S** (for Statistics). The relationship is statistically significant at the .05 level, and V is .114. So this would support our second hypothesis.

We found fairly strong support for our first hypothesis and moderate support for our second hypothesis.

Your turn.

NAME: _____

COURSE: _____

DATE: _____

EXERCISE

2b

Workbook exercises and software are copyrighted. Copying is prohibited by law.

WORKSHEET

1. Use the **SURVEY** data file and *select* the **Tabular Statistics** task.

   a. First, fill in the description of **7) OVER 50**:

   _____

   _____

   b. Use **49** or **GOV.MED.** as the row variable and **7** or **OVER 50** as the column variable. Fill in the column percentages in the following table.

   Row variable: **49) GOV.MED.**
   Column variable: **7) OVER 50**

	UNDER 50	50 & OVER
GOV'T.	%	%
SELF	%	%

   c. Describe the relationship (the pattern in the results) in this table:

   _____

   _____

   d. Cramer's V: _____

   e. Is the relationship significant at the .05 level? (Circle one.)   Yes   No

2. a. The variable 50) MUCH GOV'T directly taps opinions about government involvement in day-to-day life.

Write the description of 50) **MUCH GOV'T**:

_____

_____

_____

Using the same indicators of political conservatism as used in the exercise, test the hypothesis that conservatives are more opposed to government involvement in day-to-day life. Present the results in the following tables. (Remember to use column percentaging.)

b. Row variable: **50) MUCH GOV'T**
   Column variable: **36) POL. VIEW**

	LIBERAL	MODERATE	CONSERV.
TOO LITTLE	%	%	%
BOTH/2 MUCH	%	%	%

V = _____

Prob. = _____

c. Row variable: **50) MUCH GOV'T**
   Column variable: **39) WHO IN 92?**

	CLINTON	BUSH	PEROT
TOO LITTLE	%	%	%
BOTH/2 MUCH	%	%	%

V = _____

Prob. = _____

d. Row variable: **50) MUCH GOV'T**
   Column variable: **37) POL.PARTY**

	DEMOCRAT	INDEPENDENT	REPUBLICAN
TOO LITTLE	%	%	%
BOTH/2 MUCH	%	%	%

V = _____

Prob. = _____

e. In a few sentences, assess the results of this analysis.

3. You have opened a market research firm and your first job is to help your local art museum plan a campaign to increase attendance. The museum directors have received a donation that is to be spent on radio advertising. Your job is to select an all-music station on which to run the museum commercials. Using the **SURVEY** data set, look at variables 99 to 109—these tell us about individuals' musical preferences. Variable 111) VISIT ART tells us how often individuals visit art museums.

Select three types of music you think will be *positively* related to visiting museums. That is, the more the person likes the music, the *more likely* they are to visit museums.

(NOTE: You will notice that these tables have arrows in the corners. This means that the entire table will not fit on the screen. You must use the arrow keys to see the concealed rows and columns.)

a. Row variable: **111) VISIT ART**
   Column variable: _____

	VERY MUCH	LIKE	MIXED	DISLIKE	VERY MUCH
YES	%	%	%	%	%
NO	%	%	%	%	%

Are people who like this type of music more or less
likely to visit art museums than are individuals who
dislike this type of music?(Circle one.)   More Likely   Less Likely

b. Row variable: **111) VISIT ART**
   Column variable: _____

	VERY MUCH	LIKE	MIXED	DISLIKE	VERY MUCH
YES	%	%	%	%	%
NO	%	%	%	%	%

Are people who like this type of music more or less
likely to visit art museums than are individuals who
dislike this type of music?(Circle one.)   More Likely   Less Likely

c. Row variable: **111) VISIT ART**
   Column variable: _____

	VERY MUCH	LIKE	MIXED	DISLIKE	VERY MUCH
YES	%	%	%	%	%
NO	%	%	%	%	%

Are people who like this type of music more or less
likely to visit art museums than are individuals who
dislike this type of music?(Circle one.)   More Likely   Less Likely

Now select three types of music that you think will be *negatively* related to
visiting museums. That is, persons who like the music are *less likely* to visit
museums than are people who dislike the music.

d. Row variable: **111) VISIT ART**
   Column variable: _____

	VERY MUCH	LIKE	MIXED	DISLIKE	VERY MUCH
YES	%	%	%	%	%
NO	%	%	%	%	%

Are people who like this type of music more or less
likely to visit art museums than are individuals who
dislike this type of music?(Circle one.)   More Likely   Less Likely

e. Row variable: **111) VISIT ART**
   Column variable: _____

	VERY MUCH	LIKE	MIXED	DISLIKE	VERY MUCH
YES	%	%	%	%	%
NO	%	%	%	%	%

Are people who like this type of music more or less
likely to visit art museums than are individuals who
dislike this type of music?(Circle one.)   More Likely   Less Likely

f. Row variable: **111) VISIT ART**
   Column variable: _____

	VERY MUCH	LIKE	MIXED	DISLIKE	VERY MUCH
YES	%	%	%	%	%
NO	%	%	%	%	%

Are people who like this type of music more or less
likely to visit art museums than are individuals who
dislike this type of music?(Circle one.)   More Likely   Less Likely

g. Based on these tables, what recommendations would you make to the
   local art museum?

Evaluating Indicators

OVERVIEW

In this exercise, you'll learn more about measurement in social research. This will include further experience with different units of analysis (cases) and different levels of measurement. We also will delve more into reliability and validity, and see why we place more confidence in the accuracy of relationships among variables than we do in the accuracy of our measurements of the variables themselves.

BEFORE YOU BEGIN

Please make sure you have read Chapter 3 in the textbook and can answer the following review questions (you need not write any answers):

1. What does it mean to say that variables have variation within them?

2. Describe the levels of measurement: nominal, ordinal, interval, and ratio.

3. What are units of analysis and what are some of the different kinds of units of analysis used in social research?

4. What are aggregate data and how might misinterpretation of results based on aggregate data lead to the ecological fallacy?

5. What is reliability and what methods can we use to assess the degree of reliability of our measurements of variables?

6. What is validity and what are the common methods of assessing validity?

7. Compare and contrast indexes (or indices) and scales.

8. When using aggregate data, why is it often important to convert raw numbers (e.g., number of murders by state) into rates (e.g., murders per 100,000 population by state)?

In some of the physical sciences, measurement techniques are very sophisticated and precise because theories dictate exactly how various concepts should be measured. In the social sciences, we are not so fortunate, and a concept legitimately can be measured in many different ways. Consequently, our measures are much cruder and many ambiguities are introduced into the research process. In this exercise, we'll look at some of the special problems of measurement in social science.

UNITS OF ANALYSIS

Not all concepts used in the social sciences apply to individuals. Racial segregation, for example, refers to the extent to which two or more racial groups are separated from each other and, therefore, cannot be a property of individuals but only of *groups* of individuals. You can measure the racial segregation of cities, churches, schools, and so on, but you cannot measure the racial segregation of individuals.

Ideally, the unit of analysis used in the research hypothesis should be the same unit used in the research question. However, with some research questions, there are practical problems. For example, suicide is a relatively rare event. And since victims of suicide are not available to answer questions, studies of suicide frequently use aggregate units to test ideas.

In Exercise 2a, we were interested in the research question that hunting is a cause of violent behavior. We then looked at the relationship between the hunting license rate and indicators of violent behaviors using states as the unit of analysis. Notice that the research question deals with the individual as the unit of analysis: Are individuals who hunt more likely to behave violently than individuals who don't hunt? However, the research hypothesis uses states as the unit of analysis and looks at the connection between the hunting license rate and the murder rate. Even if the analysis at the state level had supported the research hypothesis, there would be no direct support for the underlying research question, which is trying to assess individual behavior. To do so would be to commit the ecological fallacy. When we found that the hunting license rate and the murder rates were negatively correlated, we could not necessarily conclude that they were also negatively correlated at the individual level. Similarly, we could not conclude that variables correlated at the individual level necessarily would be correlated at the aggregate level.

But even studies based on less than ideal units of analysis can contribute to knowledge. For example, based on the strong negative relationship between the hunting license rate and the murder rate that we observed, we can probably safely conclude that hunters are not *more* likely to commit murder.

AGGREGATES AND RATES

Sometimes, units or cases are combined to create an entirely new unit of analysis. Let's say, for example, that we wanted to examine the effect of the degree of school segregation on racial prejudice of students. One way to proceed with such a study would be to conduct surveys of students at schools that differed greatly in their racial composition, examine prejudice within those schools, and then compare the results across schools. For the first stage of the study (i.e., examining prejudice within schools), students would be the unit of analysis. But, when comparisons across the schools were made, schools would be the unit of analysis.

When aggregating information across individuals to obtain an aggregate measure, you always should transform the number into a rate for use in analysis. Let's take a look at what is meant by this. Start MicroCase and *open* the **USA** data file. Move to the **STATISTICAL ANALYSIS** menu, and *select* **E. Mapping Variables**. *Select* **59** or **#PLAYBOY**. When the map appears, *press* **S** (for Spot) to see the spot map. Now *press* **C** (for Compare). Use **2** or **POP 1990** as the comparison variable. Notice that the two maps are virtually identical, as shown in Figure 3.1.

Figure 3.1   Comparison of 59) #PLAYBOY and 2) POP 1990

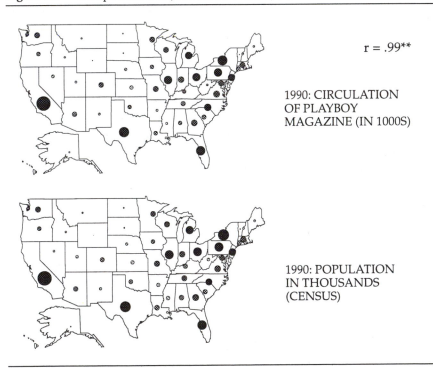

r = .99**

1990: CIRCULATION
OF PLAYBOY
MAGAZINE (IN 1000S)

1990: POPULATION
IN THOUSANDS
(CENSUS)

All we are seeing is that *Playboy* sells more copies in states with more people, which is hardly surprising. What we really want to know is which states have the highest *rates* of readership of *Playboy*. Hence, in order to make meaningful comparisons, we need to standardize across states on the basis of population. *Press <ENTER> once* and *select* **58** or **PLAYBOY**. This map shows the circulation of *Playboy*, divided by the population of the state and then multiplied by 100,000. Or put another way, this map shows the number of *Playboy* copies sold per 100,000 population. As can be seen in Figure 3.2, this map is very different from the map of raw circulation numbers.

Figure 3.2   Comparison of 59) #PLAYBOY and 58) PLAYBOY

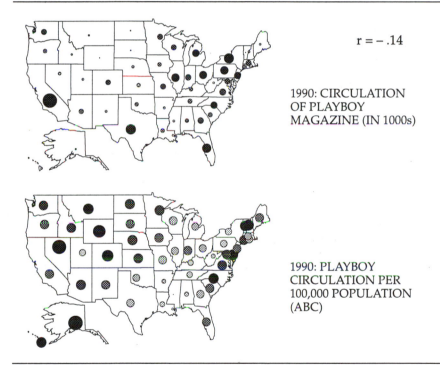

r = − .14

1990: CIRCULATION
OF PLAYBOY
MAGAZINE (IN 1000s)

1990: PLAYBOY
CIRCULATION PER
100,000 POPULATION
(ABC)

In summary, a rate is created by reducing the numbers for each unit—in this situation, each state—to a common base. Social researchers often use population as their common base, as was done in this example. This places populous states, such as California and Texas, on equal footing with states such as Wyoming and North Dakota.

LEVEL OF MEASUREMENT

Level of measurement is sometimes explained as the extent to which the categories of the variable reflect the properties of the number system. In the case of *nominal variables*, we can only sort cases into groups, such as males and females. Even if we assign a number to each group (0 for male and 1 for female), these numbers simply tell us which cases have the same gender and which cases have different genders. With *ordinal variables*, we can not only sort the cases into groups, but also order cases in terms of the property to be measured—the higher the number the more of the property possessed by the case. *Interval variables* have yet another property of true numbers—there is an equal distance between categories. *Ratio variables* not only have equal distances between categories, but also have a rational zero point. If a case is zero on a ratio variable, this case has *none* of the property being measured.

In daily life, almost all numbers we encounter (except identification numbers such as your social security number) have all of the properties of true numbers—having zero in our checking account has a very definite meaning. Unfortunately, in social science, many of the numbers we use are not really numbers—they lack one or more of the necessary properties. Therefore, we are restricted in how we can work with them. This is why the level of measurement of a variable is important. The level reflects which properties are possessed by the variable.

The numbers we assign to categories of variables, referred to as *codes*, are necessary to do quantitative social science research. But just because we are assigning numbers doesn't mean the categories actually reflect all of the properties of these numbers. If we are using a race/ethnicity variable that is coded 0 for category "white," 1 for category "African American," 2 for "Asian American," and so on, we cannot use these numbers to order cases from less to more on our race variable. We cannot say, for example, that zero represents the absence of race. We are merely using numbers to show whether cases are in the same category or in different categories.

When we analyze data, we use many different techniques, or statistics, for summarizing the observed data. Each of these techniques makes assumptions about the numeric properties possessed by the variable (i.e., its level of measurement). A frequency distribution is the simplest type of summary statistic and can be used with any level of measurement. For example, in the Introductory Exercise, we used a frequency distribution to summarize the number of people in the GSS who were males and females (a nominal variable). To do this, we simply counted the cases in each category.

Open the **SURVEY** data file and *select* the **Univariate Statistics** task. Obtain a pie chart for **45** or **RELIGION**. Notice that numbers have been assigned to the categories: Protestants are coded 1, Catholics are coded 2, and so on. This is a nominal variable, since cases can only be categorized, not ordered, by religious affiliation. *Press* **T** (for Table).

	Frequency	%	Cum. %	Z-Score
1) PROTESTANT	1025	64.2	64.2	-0.60
2) CATHOLIC	351	22.0	86.2	0.34
3) JEWISH	33	2.1	88.2	1.28
4) NONE	146	9.1	97.4	2.21
5) OTHER	42	2.6	100.0	3.15

We can see that the category Protestant has more cases than any other category. Again, do not confuse the category *code*, 1, with the number of cases in the category, 1025. *Press <ENTER>* to return to the beginning of the task.

This time use **141** or **CH.ATTEND!**. The categories of this variable are also coded with numbers: Those who never attend church are coded 0, those who attend only once a year or less often are coded 1, and so on. These codes allow us not only to group cases as similar or different, but also to order cases. So this variable is an ordinal variable. By convention, the lowest category is usually coded 1 (or 0), and the code is incremented by 1 for each additional category. *Press* **T** (for Table).

	Frequency	%	Cum. %	Z-Score
0) NEVER	259	16.5	16.5	-1.41
1) - YEAR	136	8.7	25.2	-1.05
2) 1 OR 2 YR	193	12.3	37.5	-0.69
3) SEV.A YEAR	176	11.2	48.7	-0.32
4) 1 A MONTH	112	7.1	55.9	0.04
5) 2-3 MONTH	137	8.7	64.6	0.40
6) ABOUT WKLY	99	6.3	70.9	0.77
7) WEEKLY	321	20.5	91.4	1.13
8) SEV. A WK.	135	8.6	100.0	1.49

Look at the third column labeled "Cum. %." The numbers in this column represent the percent of cases at or below that category. For example, we see that 55.9 percent attend church once a month or less often. If we couldn't order the categories, this summary measure wouldn't be valid. Looking at the previous example, we could not have said that 86.2 percent of the sample are Catholic or lower—no one would know how to interpret the statement. So cumulative percents should be used only with ordinal or higher levels of measurement.

Percentile is another word for cumulative percentage. The 90th percentile of a group on a particular variable is the category at or below which 90 percent of the group scored. The *median* is the 50th percentile. The median is a commonly used measure because it splits a sample in half—50 percent of the sample are at or below the median value.

Press <ENTER> to return to the beginning of the task. This time use **151** or **# SIBS!**. This is a ratio variable. Since the categories are ordered, the median is meaningful. In the statistics listed at the lower right of the bar graph, you can see that the median number of siblings for this sample was 2.89. This means that half of the sample had 2.9 sibs or fewer and the other half had more. (Since no one can have partial siblings, we might prefer to say that 60.8 percent had three or fewer siblings.)

Because this measure possesses equal distance between categories (a requirement of interval and ratio variables), we can add category values. Consequently, we can find the *average*, or *mean*, value of the variable. The average is found by adding the category values over all cases and dividing by the number of cases. Looking at the lower right corner, we can see that the average number of siblings for this sample was 3.68.

Both the median and the mean tell us something about the location of the middle of the distribution. Such statistics are broadly referred to as *measures of central tendency*. *Press* <ENTER> to return to the beginning of the task. Statistics that summarize the relationship *between* variables also make assumptions about the level of measurement of the variables involved. For example, in Exercise 2b, we saw that Cramer's V provides information on a cross-tabulation that is similar to the information provided by Pearson's r on a scatterplot. The main difference between these statistics and their interpretation is the level of measurement of the variables. Scatterplots and Pearson's r assume that the variables are measured at the interval or ratio level, while Cramer's V only requires nominal level of measurement.

Return to the main menu and *select* the **Tabular Statistics** task. *Select* **48** or **PRAY** as the row variable and **15** or **DEGREE** as the column variable. *Press* <ENTER> *twice* to skip the subset and control options. Row percents, column percents, and total percents can be used with nominal variables. We'll use only column percents in the exercises, so *type* **C** (for Column percentaging).

Row Variable: 48 PRAY	Column Variable: 15 DEGREE	
	DROPOUT	H.S.GRAD	SOME COL
DAILY	64.9	56.4	49.7
LESS	35.1	43.6	50.3

Press **S** (for Statistics) to see the statistics screen:

```
Nominal Statistics
Chi-Square:      11.228   DF:         2      (Prob. = 0.004)
V:               0.103    C:       0.103
Lambda(DV=15): 0.000     Lambda(DV=48): 0.004   Lambda: 0.002


Ordinal Statistics
Gamma:           0.178    Tau-b:   0.097   Tau-c:  0.106
s.err:           0.053    s.err:   0.029   s.err:  0.032


Dyx:             0.088    Dxy:     0.108
s.err.           0.026    s.err.   0.032


Prob. = 0.001
```

Notice the "Nominal Statistics" heading at the top of the screen. All the statistics in this group are appropriate for use with nominal variables. Remember that, while Cramer's V indicates the *strength* of the relationship, it does not tell us the direction or nature of the relationship. To describe the relationship, you must look at the table itself. In the middle of the screen, you will see another set of statistics: gamma, tau-b, tau-c, dyx, and dxy. As the heading suggests, these are for use with ordinal measures. Since ordinal variables (and variables with higher levels of measurement) have a natural direction or order to their categories, the relationship between variables can be either positive or negative—as one variable increases, the other variable may either increase or decrease. Hence, the statistics under this heading describe both the strength and the direction of the relationship, just as the correlation coefficient does.

Your instructor may wish you to report the value and significance of gamma when both variables are ordinal. Gamma may range from –1 through 0 to +1, where the sign shows the direction of the relationship and the value indicates the strength. The significance of gamma is shown at the bottom (Prob. = 0.001).

Be alert to the fact that MicroCase will provide values for all the statistics regardless of the level of measurement—this is true of all leading statistical packages. Consequently, in any analysis *you* must determine which statistics are appropriate. For example, it would be inappropriate to report the value of gamma for nominal variables.

As pointed out in the text, few social science variables based on individuals can be considered truly interval or ratio. For example, while years served in prison may be a ratio measure of severity of sentence, years spent in school is probably not a ratio measure of education. Unfortunately, the most powerful statistical techniques assume at least an interval level of measurement. But the use of these techniques on ordinal level variables does not seem to generate misleading conclusions in most applications, and statisticians are even finding ways to use these techniques with variables measured at the nominal level.

In this course, unless your instructor requests otherwise, we will assume that correlation and other related techniques can be used with ordinal or higher levels of measurement. You'll learn more about potential problems with this assumption when you take a statistics course.

RELIABILITY AND VALIDITY

You may have noticed that we always assess reliability by looking at the relationship *between* two variables:

- Inter-rater reliability—relationship between ratings by different individuals

- Test-retest reliability—relationship between scores on the same test at different times

- Alternate forms reliability—relationship between scores on two different forms of the same test

- Split halves reliability—relationship between scores on two different forms administered at the same time

- Internal consistency reliability—relationships among items used in an index

Let's take a quick look at Cronbach's alpha—a measure of reliability based on internal consistency. *Press* **F3** and look at the variable description for **85) FREE SPEAK**. This support for freedom of speech index is based on answers to five questions (variables 80–84) asking whether the respondent would allow a public speech by a person opposed to religion and churches, a militarist, a communist, a racist, and a homosexual.

Is this measure reliable in terms of internal consistency? It is possible that some of these questions are reliable indicators while others are not. While social scientists usually focus more on validity than on reliability, let's look at one common measure of reliability that could be used here: Cronbach's alpha coefficient. Alpha is used to measure internal consistency—based on the extent to which the items are correlated with one another—especially when a researcher is developing an index to measure some concept.

Cronbach's alpha varies from 0 (completely unreliable) to 1.0 (perfectly reliable in terms of internal consistency). If alpha is 0.7 or higher, then the index is reliable.

Return to the **STATISTICAL ANALYSIS** menu and *select* the **Correlation** task. For variable 1, *select* **80** or **ATHEIST SP** and *press* *<ENTER>*. For variable 2, *select* **81** or **RACIST SPK** and *press* *<ENTER>*. For variable 3, *select* **82** or **COMMUN SPK** and *press* *<ENTER>*. For variable 4, *select* **83** or **MILITI. SP** and *press <ENTER>*. For variable 5, *select* **84** or **GAY SPEAK** and *press <ENTER> three times.*

```
Cronbach's alpha:  0.828
                  80) ATHEIST SP  81) RACIST SPK  82) COMMUN SPK 83) MILITI. SP
80) ATHEIST SP        1.000           0.561**         0.593**        0.526**
81) RACIST SPK        0.561**         1.000           0.446**        0.478**
82) COMMUN SPK        0.593**         0.446**         1.000          0.563**
83) MILITI. SP        0.526**         0.478**         0.563**        1.000
84) GAY SPEAK         0.477*          0.347**         0.478**        0.448**


                  84) GAY SPEAK
80) ATHEIST SP        0.477**
81) RACIST SPK        0.347**
82) COMMUN SPK        0.478**
83) MILITI. SP        0.448**
84) GAY SPEAK         1.000
```

At the top of the screen, you can see that Cronbach's alpha is 0.828 and hence our index is reliable. You can see that this high value results from the high correlations among the component variables.

Similarly, all tests of validity, except face validity, are also based on examining the relationship between variables. For example, in the **SURVEY** data set, individuals are asked how often they go to church and also how religious they are. If the measure of religiosity is valid, we would expect that those who go to church more often would be more religious. So we could look at the relationship between these variables to test the validity of the religiosity measure. Using the **Tabular Statistics** task, *select* **47** or **HOW RELIG?** as the row variable and **46** or **CH.ATTEND** as the column variable. When the table appears, *press* **C** (for Column percentaging).

```
        Row variable: 47) HOW RELIG?   Column variable: 46) CH.ATTEND

                           NOT OFTEN              OFTEN
        STRONG               17.2                 67.3
        LESS                 82.8                 32.7


        Cramer's V = 0.508
        Prob. = 0.000
```

We can see that those who attend church often claim to be more religious than those who don't. Hence, we have more confidence in the validity of our measure of religiosity.

WHY RELATIONSHIPS?

This focus on relationships is also a result of the crudeness of our measures. Very few social science variables have categories that allow us to give meaningful interpretations to the distribution of a single variable. Generally, only variables with "natural" categories, such as sex, race, and political party affiliation, or variables measured at the ratio level, such as age and income, provide meaningful distributions. For example, the statement that a group is 70 percent female or the statement that the average age of the group is 63.5 can be unambiguously interpreted. However, distributions of single variables that have a natural continuum but no meaningful zero point, such as degree of belief in God, attitude toward abortion, or degree of confidence in the government, cannot be interpreted easily. For example, the statement that 60 percent of the population has a great deal of confidence in the government has little meaning. How much is a "great deal"? We don't know whether this is higher or lower than the confidence held for other groups, such as big business and labor unions, or even whether confidence in government is higher or lower than it was last year or 10 years ago.

Analysis of individual variables is also problematic since relatively minor changes in the wording of questions may have sizable effects on the distribution of responses. In the **SURVEY** data file, some questions have alternate wordings, and half the sample (randomly selected) was asked one version and half was asked the other. This was a methodological study to determine how much changes in question wordings would affect the responses. *Select* the **Univariate Statistics** task and obtain the distribution for **54** or **BIG CITY $**. After the pie chart appears, *press* **T** (for Table).

```
            Spending on solving the problems of the big
            cities.

            TOO LITTLE            61.6
            RIGHT                 25.1
            TOO MUCH              13.2
```

Examine the question wording and the percentage distributions for a moment. Then *press* <ENTER> to return to the start of the **Univariate Statistics** task and *use* **65** or **BIG CITY$2** as the variable. After the pie chart appears, *press* **T** (for Table).

```
            Spending on assistance to big cities.

            TOO LITTLE            27.7
            RIGHT                 35.9
            TOO MUCH              36.4
```

What may seem like slight changes in question wording had a huge effect on the percentage who selected each category. When asked about assistance to big cities, only 27.7 percent thought the government was spending too little, but when asked about solving the problems of the big cities, 61.6 percent thought too little was being spent. Before seeing the data, almost any researcher would have accepted these questions as interchangeable indicators of the respondent's attitude toward subsidies of large cities. After we see the data, we can, of course, speculate on how these questions must be tapping somewhat different attitudes, but such *ex post facto* analysis will not help us design indicators for another concept. If such minor changes in wording will make such a big change in the resulting distribution, how can social scientists ever develop adequate indicators of concepts?

Fortunately, as social scientists, we are primarily interested in the *relationship* between variables. It turns out that relationships between variables are usually much less sensitive than distributions of simple variables to changes in measurement techniques. Despite their limitations as descriptions, both of these question wordings are useful for comparing across groups. For example, we could use this variable to test the hypothesis that urban residents will want to spend more on city problems than will rural residents. Switch back to the **Tabular Statistics** task and use **54** or **BIG CITY $** as the row variable and **9** or **URBAN?** as the column variable. *Press* **C** (for Column percentaging).

Row variable: 54) BIG CITY $ Column variable: 9) URBAN?

	URBAN	RURAL
TOO LITTLE	63.2	53.9
RIGHT	25.8	21.7
TOO MUCH	11.0	24.3

Cramer's V = 0.149
Prob. = 0.000

Compare the percentages of people from urban and rural areas who think too little is being done to solve the problems of big cities. Now make **65** or **BIG CITY$2** the row variable and **9** or **URBAN?** the column variable and use column percentaging. This table will appear:

Row variable: 65) BIG CITY$2   Column variable: 9) URBAN?

	URBAN	RURAL
TOO LITTLE	29.6	18.0
RIGHT	35.9	34.0
TOO MUCH	34.6	48.0

Cramer's V = 0.114
Prob. = 0.016

Compare the two groups again. Notice that, regardless of the wording difference, the *relationship* between area of residence and attitude toward spending on big cities is the same. Our hypothesis would be supported with either variable: Urban residents are more likely than rural residents to think too little is being spent on big cities, and the results are statistically significant.

Studies that examine changes over time are also looking at relationships—time is one of the variables. For example, if we compare the distribution of attitudes toward spending on big cities in 1972 with the distribution of this attitude in 1992, we are looking at the effect of "time" on this attitude. Of course, for such a comparison to be valid, the same measure of attitude toward spending on big cities must be used each time.

Your turn.

NAME: _____

COURSE: _____

DATE: _____

EXERCISE

3

Workbook exercises and software are copyrighted. Copying is prohibited by law.

WORKSHEET

1. *Open* the **SURVEY** data file and look at the descriptions for the following variables. For each variable, indicate the level of measurement by circling *nominal, ordinal,* or *interval/ratio*. Be sure to examine the categories used with each variable.

131) ZODIAC	Nominal	Ordinal	Interval/ratio
143) PRAY!	Nominal	Ordinal	Interval/ratio
5) REGION	Nominal	Ordinal	Interval/ratio
36) POL. VIEW	Nominal	Ordinal	Interval/ratio
53) HEALTH $	Nominal	Ordinal	Interval/ratio
99) BIG BAND	Nominal	Ordinal	Interval/ratio

2. Different kinds of research require different kinds of units of analysis (cases). For each of the following research questions, circle *yes* if it would be appropriate to use individuals as the units of analysis (cases) or *no* if it would not be appropriate.

a. Are racial attitudes of people related to their education levels? (Circle one.)   Yes   No

b. Does state spending on education reduce the crime rate? (Circle one.)   Yes   No

c. Does economic development in nations lead to more democratic political institutions? (Circle one.)   Yes   No

d. Are older people more supportive of Social Security than younger people are? (Circle one.)   Yes   No

e. Do sports fans tend to be more socially active than people who are not sports fans? (Circle one.)   Yes   No

3. In the Canadian General Social Survey conducted by Statistics Canada, the following question asks respondents about church attendance:

Other than on special occasions, such as weddings, funerals or baptisms, how often did you attend services or meetings connected with your religion in the last 12 months?
Was it . . .
At least once a week?
At least once a month?
A few times a year?
At least once a year?
Not at all

a. Using the **SURVEY** data set, record the variable description and answer categories for **46) CH.ATTEND**.
Description:

_____

_____

Categories:

b. What concept is being measured by these two variables?

c. Which of these church attendance items is the better indicator? Why?

d. Record the description and answer categories of **141) CH.ATTEND!**.
Description:

_____

_____

Categories:

e. Let's compare the strengths and weaknesses of
this indicator with the one used by Statistics Canada.
Which one allows for the measurement of greater
variation? (Circle one.)   141) CH.ATTEND!

Statistics Canada question

f. Which one appears to be better at measuring the
frequency with which people *ordinarily* attend
religious services? (Circle one.)   141) CH.ATTEND!

Statistics Canada question

4. a. What is the description for **129) INTERMAR?**

_____

_____

b. What concept do you think this variable is measuring?

c. What is the description for **130) RACE SEG.?**

_____

_____

_____

d. Go to the **STATISTICAL ANALYSIS** menu and *select* the **Tabular
Statistics** task. Use **129** or **INTERMAR?** as the row variable and **130** or
RACE SEG. as the column variable. Use column percentaging and fill in
the following table:

Row variable: **129) INTERMAR?**
Column variable: **130) RACE SEG.**

	AGREE STR.	AG.SLIGHT	DIS.SLIGHT	DISAGR.STR
YES	%	%	%	%
NO	%	%	%	%

e. Let us assume for the moment that 130) RACE SEG is a
   fairly valid measure of the concept you just specified. Based
   on this table, how valid is variable 129) INTERMAR?
   in measuring this same concept? (Circle one.)

                                                        Very valid
                                                    Somewhat valid
                                                     Not very valid

Explain your answer.

5. Using the **Univariate Statistics** task, find the percentages of survey respondents who would allow an abortion in each of the situations specified in
   variables 73–78 and write these percentages in the blanks provided.

   73) ABORT DEF   _____%

   74) ABORT WANT   _____%

   75) ABORT HLTH   _____%

   76) ABORT NO$ _____%

   77) ABORT RAPE   _____%

   78) ABORT SIGL   _____%

   Now, based on these results, discuss the following statement: "Most
   Americans approve of abortion. In a recent national random sample of
   adults, over 89% approved of abortion."

6. In addition to 54) BIG CITY $ and 65) BIG CITY$2 discussed in this exercise, alternate wordings of several other variables were included in the methodological study for **SURVEY**.

    Provide the variable description and distribution for each of the following variables:

    a. **52) ENVIRON. $**
       Description:

    _____

    _____

    In the table below, fill in the appropriate frequency and percentage distributions.

	FREQUENCY	%
TOO LITTLE		
RIGHT		
TOO MUCH		

    b. **63) ENVIRON.$2**
       Description:

    _____

    _____

Again, fill in the table below.

	FREQUENCY	%
TOO LITTLE		
RIGHT		
TOO MUCH		

c. Compare the results for these two variables. Do you
   think it is legitimate to consider these two variables
   as indicators of the same concept? (Circle one.)   Yes   No

d. If you answered YES, provide a definition of the concept. If you answered
   NO, provide definitions of the two concepts being measured.

e. Now use **Tabular Statistics** to examine the relationship between **115)
   VEGETARIAN** and each of these environmental variables. The hypothesis is: Vegetarians are more likely to think too little is being spent on the
   environment than are nonvegetarians.

   Use **52** or **ENVIRON. $** as the row variable and **115** or **VEGETARIAN** as
   the column variable. Provide column percentages.

	VEGETARIAN	EATS MEAT
TOO LITTLE	%	%
RIGHT	%	%
TOO MUCH	%	%

V = _____

Prob. = _____

Is the hypothesis supported or rejected?
(Circle one.)   Supported   Rejected

f. Use **63** or **ENVIRON.$2** as the row variable and **115** or **VEGETARIAN** as the column variable. Provide column percentages.

	VEGETARIAN	EATS MEAT
TOO LITTLE	%	%
RIGHT	%	%
TOO MUCH	%	%

V = _____

Prob. = _____

Is the hypothesis supported or rejected?
(Circle one.)   Supported   Rejected

7. Another set of variables with alternative wording in the **SURVEY** file is 55) CRIME$ and 66) CRIME $2. Provide the description and distribution for each of the following:

a. **55) CRIME $**
   Description:

   _____

   _____

   Distribution:

	FREQUENCY	%
TOO LITTLE		
RIGHT		
TOO MUCH		

b. **66) CRIME $2**
   Description:

   _____

   _____

Distribution:

	FREQUENCY	%
TOO LITTLE		
RIGHT		
TOO MUCH		

c. Compare the results for these two variables. Do you think it is legitimate to consider these two variables as indicators of the same concept? (Circle one.)   Yes   No

d. If you answered YES, provide a definition of the concept. If you answered NO, provide definitions of the two concepts being measured.

8. Now test the hypothesis that there will be a relationship between **13) FEAR WALK** and each of these crime spending variables. The hypothesis is: Those who are afraid to walk alone at night are more likely to think too little is being spent on crime spending than are individuals who are not afraid.

a. Use **55** or **CRIME $** as the row variable and **13** or **FEAR WALK** as the column variable. Provide column percentages.

	YES	NO
TOO LITTLE	%	%
RIGHT	%	%
TOO MUCH	%	%

V = _____

Prob. = _____

Is the hypothesis supported or rejected?
(Circle one.)   Supported   Rejected

b. Use **66** or **CRIME $2** as the row variable and **13** or **FEAR WALK** as the column variable. Provide column percentages.

	YES	NO
TOO LITTLE		
RIGHT		
TOO MUCH		

V = _____

Prob. = _____

Is the hypothesis supported or rejected?
(Circle one.)   Supported   Rejected

4

Selecting Cases

OVERVIEW

In this exercise, you will learn more about problems that can cause bias in samples, and you will also see that some sampling problems probably do not seriously distort the accuracy of the results.

BEFORE YOU BEGIN

Please make sure you have read Chapter 4 in the textbook and can answer the following review questions (you need not write any answers):

1. What is the difference between a census and a sample?

2. What is the difference between a parameter and a statistic?

3. If the confidence interval for a sample is plus or minus 3 percentage points and the confidence level is 95 percent, what does this mean in terms of the results?

4. Suppose you have a list of all students in your college and you want to take a sample of them. How would you go about selecting (a) a simple random sample and (b) a systematic random sample?

5. Describe the general process by which you would select a probability sample of people in a city for a telephone survey.

6. Describe how each of the following sources of bias can distort random samples: nonresponse bias, selective availability bias, areal bias.

7. What is a SLOPS and how trustworthy are the results of such surveys?

The first step in selecting cases is to define the relevant population. When one is primarily interested in *describing* a particular group of units, determining the population is straightforward. A magazine, for example, might be interested in the opinions of its current subscribers; the appropriate population is individuals who subscribe to the magazine. Or a college might want to determine how its students budget their time; students enrolled at the school would be the population of interest. A city might want to evaluate the utilization of recreational facilities; the available facilities might be used as the cases.

When research shifts to *testing ideas* rather than describing groups, defining the appropriate population is not so easy. For example, a researcher testing a theory about the effect of organizational structure on decision making would probably want to define the relevant population as all organizations over all time. Similarly, someone interested in the effect of new and contradictory information on attitude change might want to generalize the results to all humans over all time. Clearly, however, there is no way to take a census of either of these populations or even to draw scientific samples. Consequently, researchers settle for working with a subset of the population of interest. For example, the organization researcher might define the population as all business firms within a particular geographic area at the current time. The attitude change researcher might define the population as individuals over age 18 currently residing in the United States. Other researchers testing these same theories might choose quite different populations. In fact, one type of replication research is to test the same hypotheses in a different population. Thus, a researcher might replicate the organizational study by using national charitable organizations as the relevant population.

Having defined the appropriate population, the next step is to determine how cases are to be selected from this population. For many research questions, using a census of the units is more appropriate than selecting a sample. If an instructor were interested in the opinions and attitudes of students in a particular class, he or she should simply take a census of the class—that is, include all members in the study. There is no reason to select a sample, since the entire population is accessible and relatively small—why introduce unnecessary sources of inaccuracy? If one is studying state governments, governments of all 50 states would be included, unless the data collection process was quite complicated. In short, samples are used only when taking a census would be more difficult.

If a sample is to be used, researchers must determine how to select the sample. If we wish to generalize the results from the sample to the population, then we must use a probability (or random) sample. With such samples, we can determine the exact probability that a particular case in the population is included in the sample. Using probability theory, we can then generalize from the observed sample to the population. This process of inferring from a sample to a population will be covered in detail when you take a statistics course. For now, you can simply assume that, when a proper sample is selected, the sample statistic pro-vides the best estimate of the population parameter. For example, if the propor-tion of females in the sample is .63 (sample statistic), then our best estimate of the proportion of females in the population is .63 (population parameter).

An important property of probability samples is that two or more random samples of the same population can be combined and this combined sample is also a probability sample. This can be very useful. Suppose, for example, you find that a substantial number of cases in your sample are no longer members of the selected population—perhaps they have moved to an area not included in your sampling frame. As a result, your sample will have many fewer cases than you had planned. You can replace these cases by simply drawing another sample, including sufficient cases to complete the original sample, and combine these data with your first sample (you would, of course, want to drop any duplicates that appear).

The problem with an *improperly* selected sample is that estimates of the pop-ulation parameters are almost certain to be incorrect. Let's look at an example. Suppose you administered a survey to those attending Sunday services at several churches. Start MicroCase and *open* the **SURVEY** data set. *Select* the **Univariate** task and *select* **46** or **CH.ATTEND** as your variable. Do not select a subset, and *press* **D** (for Distribution) when the pie chart appears. The following distribution will appear on the screen:

	FREQUENCY	%
NOT OFTEN	876	55.9
OFTEN	692	44.1

Unless some unusual Sunday is selected, we would expect less than half the pop-ulation to be in church.

But the real problem is that those who are in church will differ in many ways from those not in church. Let's look at some of these differences. Return to the beginning of the task and use **1** or **SEX**. *Press* **D** (for Distribution).

	FREQUENCY	%
MALE	685	42.7
FEMALE	921	57.3

The percentage of males in the total sample is 42.7. Now let's look at the sex dis-tribution of church attenders. Return to the beginning of the task and again *select* **1** or **SEX**. But this time when you are asked about a subset, *select* **46** or **CH.ATTEND**. *Type* **2** when asked for the lower limit and *type* **2** again when asked for the upper limit. *Press* <ENTER> when asked about a second subset. The result-ing pie chart contains information on only those who were coded 2 on 46) CH.ATTEND—those who attended church often. *Press* **T** (for Table).

46) CH.ATTEND (Subset with value often)

	FREQUENCY	%
MALE	248	35.8
FEMALE	444	64.2

Among those who attend church frequently, only 35.8 percent are males. So we see one way in which this sample is quite biased: Males are likely to be underrepresented. We can think of several other ways in which this sample, which was selected from people attending Sunday services, will probably be biased. We might expect younger individuals who are single to be underrepresented. Or perhaps individuals from different regions will be differentially represented.

Even if you selected a proper probability sample of churchgoers, you could not generalize your results to the general population. In fact, if you simply collected data at some churches or collected data on a particular Sunday, you would not have a proper sample of churchgoers and you could not even generalize your results to churchgoers.

Another form of sampling bias can result from the type of interviewing process that is selected. Some surveys, such as the U.S. General Social Survey, use face-to-face interviews, while other surveys use telephone interviews. Let's see if there is any serious bias generated by using telephone interviews. *Select* the **Univariate** task and *select* **26** or **PHONE.**

	FREQUENCY	%
NO PHONE	143	8.9
PHONE	1463	91.1

We can see that 143 cases—about 9 percent of the sample—did not have a phone. If NORC had conducted phone interviews rather than personal interviews, they would not have been able to reach these individuals who didn't have phones. Who are we likely to undersample if we select only cases who have telephones? Perhaps those with low incomes would be undersampled, since they are probably somewhat less likely to have telephones. Let's first look at the distribution of income in the total sample. Use **22** or **R.INCOME** and *press* **T** (for Table).

	FREQUENCY	%
UNDER 15K	344	33.8
15K-29999K	345	33.9
30K & OVER	330	32.4

As we can see, each category has about one-third of the sample. Now let's see what will happen if we look at the income distribution of only those individuals who have telephones. To do this, we'll use the subset feature of MicroCase. Return to the beginning of the task. Again *select* **22)** or **R.INCOME.** When asked for the variable to be used for a subset, *select* **26** or **PHONE**. We want to look at only those who have telephones, so *enter* **1** when asked for the low value and *enter* **1** again when asked for the high value. *Press <ENTER>* in response to the next prompt. Now only cases with phones will be included in the distribution. *Press* **T** (for Table).

26) PHONE (Subset with value phone)

	FREQUENCY	%
UNDER 15K	306	32.5
15K-29999K	326	34.6
30K & OVER	309	32.8

We can see that excluding cases with no telephone makes only a small difference in the income distribution. For example, the percentage in the lowest income category changes from 33.8 to 32.5, or slightly over 1 percentage point.

Similarly we might expect older individuals to be undersampled in a phone survey. Return to the beginning of the task and *select* **7** or **OVER 50**. Look at the distribution of age in the total sample.

	FREQUENCY	%
UNDER 50	1013	63.3
50 & OVER	588	36.7

Let's now look at the distribution of age among those respondents with telephones. Again *select* **7** or **OVER 50**. When asked for a subset, use **26 PHONE** and *use* **1** as both the lower and upper limit. *Press <ENTER>* when asked for the second subset variable.

26) PHONE (Subset with value phone)

	FREQUENCY	%
UNDER 50	911	62.4
50 & OVER	550	37.6

Again, when individuals with phones are excluded, the change is less than 1 percentage point in either of these categories. This suggests that conducting interviews over the telephone rather than using personal interviews would not have a serious effect on the results, assuming that a proper probability sample were selected (and that the nonresponse rate did not substantially increase).

Bias also can be introduced when cases selected for the sample refuse to participate. For example, in the 1994 General Social Survey, 854 individuals in the selected sample failed to complete the interview for one reason or another. To the extent that these individuals differ from those who completed the interview, the sample will be biased. Or, if a sizable number of individuals refuses to answer a particular question, any analysis involving that question may fail to reflect the population parameters. Occasionally, individuals are dropped because their answers are clearly frivolous. Sometimes, interviews are not completed because respondents become too hostile or are obviously incapable of understanding the questions. In telephone interviews, a respondent may simply hang up in the middle of the interview.

In order to help identify cases who may be providing incorrect answers, interviewers are frequently asked to provide information about the general ambience of the interview. For example, the interviewers for the GSS were asked to rate each respondent's level of comprehension. Return to the beginning of the **Univariate Statistics** task. *Select* **127** or **COMPREHEND** and *press* **T** (for Table).

	FREQUENCY	%
GOOD	1310	81.9
FAIR	240	15.0
POOR	49	3.1

Only a small percent (3.1%) of respondents had difficulty understanding the questions. The likely effect of retaining individuals with poor understanding is introducing random "noise" into the survey—their answers are more likely to contain a random component than are answers of other respondents. Return to the beginning of the task.

In addition, interviewers were asked to report whether respondents were cooperative or hostile. *Select* **128** or **ATTITUDE?** and *press* **T** (for Table).

	FREQUENCY	%
FRIENDLY	1271	79.3
COOPERATIV	261	16.3
IMPAT/HOST	70	4.4

The percent who were impatient or hostile is also very small.

You should realize that even a properly selected sample will not be perfectly accurate in estimating population parameters. Generalizing from samples to population is a probablistic, not a deterministic, process. For example, based on the GSS sample, our best estimate of the percent of males in the population is 42.7. Even if the response rate had been perfect, the true population parameter would likely be somewhat different from this estimate. If we select another sample of 1,606 cases using similar procedures, the percent of males is likely to be slightly different. If we select yet another sample, we will get yet another estimate. In a statistics course, you will learn how to evaluate the accuracy of such estimates.

Your turn.

NAME: _____

COURSE: _____

DATE: _____

Workbook exercises and software are copyrighted. Copying is prohibited by law.

EXERCISE

4

WORKSHEET

1. A researcher wanted to generalize from his survey results to the population that had received a questionnaire. When asked if the returned questionnaires could be considered a random sample of the population, he replied, "We sent out 100,000 questionnaires and got only 5,000 back. What could be more random than that?" Is he right? Why or why not?

2. Suppose that, instead of selecting a random sample and using telephone or personal interviews, you decided to find your respondents at the local tavern. Using the **SURVEY** data, we can see how those who go to bars once a week or more often differ from those who don't go to bars. *Open* the **SURVEY** data file and *select* the **Univariate Statistics** task.

   a. *Select* **29** or **SOC. BAR** and fill in the following table:

	FREQUENCY	%
2+/MONTH		
1–/MONTH		

   What percentage of the total sample goes to bars twice a month or more?

b. Perhaps females would be undersampled. First *select* **1** or **SEX** and fill in the following table:

	FREQUENCY	%
MALE		
FEMALE		

In the total sample, what is the percentage of females? _____

c. Let's compare the distribution of sex in the total sample with the subset who frequent bars. *Select* **1** or **SEX** and *use* **29** or **SOC. BAR** as the subset variable. Use **1** as the lower limit and **1** as the upper limit to select only those cases who go to bars frequently. Fill in the following table:

SUBSET WITH VALUE 2+/MONTH

	FREQUENCY	%
MALE		
FEMALE		

Among those who go to bars frequently, what is the percentage of females?

_____

What does this suggest about the distribution of sex among a sample drawn from local taverns?

d. People who frequent bars probably differ in many other ways from the general population. Select one variable that you think will differ and conduct a similar analysis:

Name of the variable: _____

Description of the variable:

_____

_____

Provide the distribution of the variable in the *total* sample—use only as many rows as necessary:

	FREQUENCY	%

e. Obtain the distribution of the variable in the subset that goes to bars frequently. In addition to filling in the results below, attach a printout (*press* **P**) of your analysis. (If your computer is not connected to a printer or if you have been instructed not to use the printer, just skip these printing instructions.)

SUBSET WITH VALUE 2+/MONTH

	FREQUENCY	%

Discuss the implications of these results for obtaining your respondents from taverns.

3. a. Let's see if the distribution of educational attainment would be affected if only individuals with telephones were included in the sample. *Select* the **Univariate** task and *select* **15** or **DEGREE**. Fill in the following table for this distribution:

	FREQUENCY	%
NOT HI SCH		
HIGH SCH		
SOME COLL.		

b. Now repeat this analysis using **26** or **PHONE** as the subset variable. (Limit analysis to category 1—have phone.)

SUBSET WITH VALUE PHONE

	FREQUENCY	%
NOT HI SCH		
HIGH SCH		
SOME COLL.		

Describe how using phone interviews rather than personal interviews would affect the distribution of education in the observed sample:

c. Select another variable from the **SURVEY** data file that may be affected by whether telephone or personal interviews are used. (Use different variables than those used earlier in this exercise.)

Variable name: _____

Variable description:

_____

_____

Fill in the distribution for the total sample in the table below:

	FREQUENCY	%

d. Now fill in the distribution for the subset with telephones. In addition, attach a printout (*press* **P**) of your analysis. (If your computer is not connected to a printer or if you have been instructed not to use the printer, just skip these printing instructions.)

SUBSET WITH VALUE PHONE

	FREQUENCY	%

Describe how the distribution of this variable would differ depending upon which type of interview was used.

4. a. *Select* the **Tabular Statistics** task, and make **15** or **DEGREE** the row variable and *select* **127** or **COMPREHEND** as the column variable. Use column percentaging to complete the following table:

	GOOD	FAIR	POOR
NOT HI SCHOOL	%	%	%
HIGH SCH	%	%	%
SOME COLL.	%	%	%

   b. *Select* **15** or **DEGREE** as the row variable and **128** or **ATTITUDE?** as the column variable. Use column percentaging to complete the following table:

	FRIENDLY	COOPERATIV	IMPAT/HOST
NOT HI SCHOOL	%	%	%
HIGH SCH	%	%	%
SOME COLL.	%	%	%

Assuming that individuals who are hostile or impatient or who fail to understand the questions are the most likely to break off an interview, how would the distribution of educational attainment in the sample be affected?

5a

Control Variables

OVERVIEW

In the first part of this exercise, you will learn how to examine a relationship between two variables while controlling for the effects of another variable—and you will see why this is important when we try to disentangle relationships among variables. In the second part, you will gain experience in using regression to examine the simultaneous effects of two or more independent variables on a dependent variable, and you will see how this is useful in assessing models of what causes the dependent variable.

BEFORE YOU BEGIN

Please make sure you have read Chapter 5 in the textbook and can answer the following review questions (you need not write any answers):

1. Describe the three criteria of causation (time order, etc.).

2. How are independent, dependent, intervening, and antecedent variables related to each other?

3. What does multiple causation mean?

4. What are causal models and how is regression used in assessing causal models?

5. If the beta coefficient for an independent variable in regression is .50, what does this mean? (Assume that it is statistically significant.)

6. If a squared multiple regression correlation (R^2) is .80, what does this mean?

7. How can regression be useful in identifying spurious relationships?

8. How can regression help in sorting out the effects of suppressor variables?

9. What are dummy variables and how are they used in regression?

Before we look at control variables in cross-tabulation, let's take a closer look at the variables we'll be using. Start MicroCase. *Open* the **SURVEY** data file and *select* the **Tabular Statistics** task. *Select* **138** or **R.INCOME!** as the row variable and **22** or **R.INCOME** as the column variable. Do not select a subset or control variables, and do *not* percentage the resulting table:

FREQUENCIES
Row Variable: 138) R.INCOME!   Column Variable: 22) R.INCOME

	UNDER 15K	15K-29999K	30K & OVER	Missing	TOTAL
UNDER 1K	26	0	0	0	26
1K-2999	38	0	0	0	38
3K-3999	33	0	0	0	33
4K-4999	28	0	0	0	28
5K-5999	24	0	0	0	24
6K-6999	25	0	0	0	25
7K-7999	16	0	0	0	16
8K-9999	34	0	0	0	34
10K-12499	62	0	0	0	62
12.5-14999	58	0	0	0	58
15K-17499	0	69	0	0	69
17.5-19999	0	63	0	0	63
20K-22499	0	57	0	0	57
22.5-24999	0	66	0	0	66
25K-29999	0	90	0	0	90
30K-34999	0	0	89	0	89
35K-39999	0	0	61	0	61
40K-49999	0	0	70	0	70
50K-59999	0	0	38	0	38
60K-74999	0	0	25	0	25
75K AND UP	0	0	47	0	47
Missing	0	0	0	587	587
TOTAL	344	345	330	587	1019

Variable 22) R INCOME is based on exactly the same question as variable 138) R. INCOME!. The only difference is that variable 138 includes all answer categories made available to respondents for reporting their own annual income, whereas variable 22 was created by combining a number of these categories. The table shows you which categories of 138) R.INCOME! have been combined to form the categories for 22) R.INCOME. For example, categories from UNDER 1K to 12.5-14999 on variable 138) R.INCOME! were placed in the category UNDER 15K on variable 22) R.INCOME. This is called *collapsing* the variable—22) R.INCOME is a *collapsed* version of 138) R.INCOME! (in this data set all variables with an exclamation point are uncollapsed versions of variables; many of these also are included in a collapsed form). Collapsing seems to go against the idea of trying to have as

much variation as possible in our variables since variable 22 has only three categories while variable 138 has 21. Why do we do this?

Return to the beginning of the task and *select* **138** or **R.INCOME!** as the row variable and **135** or **EDUCATION!** as the column variable. Again skip the control and subset options. This time *select* **Column percentaging.** You will need to use the arrow keys to move around in this huge table. Even a very experienced professional analyst would not be able to make much sense of this table. Many of the columns have very few cases, so the percentages for the most part are meaningless. This is why we collapse variables when using tabular analysis—to get enough cases in the categories to be able to interpret the results. Because we will be using cross-tabulation in this exercise, virtually all of the variables are in collapsed form. While collapsing will change the *distribution* of the variable, such changes rarely affect *relationships* with other variables as we saw in Exercise 2b. (In Chapter 7, you'll learn the principles of collapsing variables.)

Now let's look at an example of a spurious relationship. Return to the beginning of the task and create a table using **32** or **SEX FREQ** as the row variable and **4** or **MARITAL** as the independent variable. Select column percentaging.

```
Row Variable: 32) SEX FREQ    Column Variable: 4) MARITAL

                  MARRIED      DIV/WIDOWD     NEV.MARRY
  -MONTHLY          12.1          56.1          32.0
  MONTHLY+          87.9          43.9          68.0

  N                 759           394           275
```

The row variable tells us how often a respondent has had sex during the previous 12 months. In this form, the variable has been collapsed into those who had sex less often than once a month and those who had sex at least once a month or more often. It should surprise no one that married people were more apt to have sex at least once a month than were people in the other two categories. However, it does seem unusual that the difference between the never married and the widowed and divorced group should be so great. Let's just focus on those two groups.

First, let's use subsetting to eliminate the married individuals. *Select* **32** or **SEX FREQ** as the row variable and **4** or **MARITAL** as the column variable. Do not select a control variable. Select a subset based on **4** or **MARITAL**, and use **2** as the lower limit and **3** as the upper limit. Use column percentaging.

```
SUBSET BETWEEN DIV/WIDOWD and NEV.MARRY ON MARITAL
Row Variable: 32) SEX FREQ    Column Variable: 4) MARITAL

                  DIV/WIDOWD     NEV.MARRY
  -MONTHLY          56.1          32.0
  MONTHLY+          43.9          68.0

  N                 394           275
```

We can now focus on the difference between these two groups. This table shows a percentage difference of 24.1 in the first row, and the N's (number of cases) reported at the bottom are large enough that we can have some confidence in the stability of the percentages. *Press* **S** (for Statistics). Cramer's V is .238 and is highly significant.

We have now observed a relationship between marital status and frequency of sex among those who are not married. But could this relationship be spurious? Is there some other variable that could be creating this difference? If so, this other variable must precede these two variables in time. Perhaps age might be this variable. Age has an effect on both of these variables—the never-married group is probably younger and younger individuals are probably more likely to have sex.

Let's diagram this argument:

AMONG THE NOT MARRIED

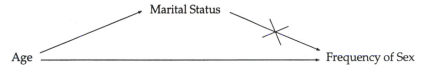

The position of the variables from left to right indicates time order. The arrows indicate causal relationships. The arrow at the right with the X across it represents a relationship that disappears when we control for age. Now let's test this argument by controlling for age.

Return to the beginning of the task. *Select* **32** or **SEX FREQ** as the row variable, **4** or **MARITAL** as the column variable, and **7** or **OVER 50** as the control variable. Do not select a second control variable, but again use subsetting to limit the results to the categories of *2* and *3* on *4)* MARITAL. The first table will show the relationship between marital status and frequency of sex for those under 50. Use column percentaging.

```
SUBSET BETWEEN DIV/WIDOWD and NEV.MARRY ON MARITAL
Control Category: UNDER 50
Row Variable: 32) SEX FREQ      Column Variable: 4) MARITAL

                   DIV/WIDOWD      NEV.MARRY
    -MONTHLY          26.5           26.8
    MONTHLY+          73.5           73.2

    N                 185            250
```

There is no difference between these two groups among those under 50. *Press* **S** (for Statistics). You'll see that Cramer's V is .004 and clearly not significant. *Press* **T** (for Table) to return to the table. *Press* *<ENTER> once* to see the table for those 50 and over. Use column percentaging.

```
SUBSET BETWEEN DIV/WIDOWD and NEV.MARRY ON MARITAL
Control Category: 50 & OVER
Row Variable: 32) SEX FREQ     Column Variable: 4) MARITAL

                    DIV/WIDOWD      NEV.MARRY
-MONTHLY               82.2           83.3
MONTHLY+               17.8           16.7

N                      208             24
```

This table shows no difference for those 50 and over. *Press* **S** (for Statistics)and *press* <ENTER> to close the window that warns about a chi-square problem. Cramer's V is .009 and not significant. The relationship between marital status (excluding married individuals) and frequency of sex would appear to be spurious, produced by variations in age. Widowed and divorced persons do not have sex less frequently than do never-married people *in their age group*! The initial differences between the groups are the result of the fact that, as a group, people who are widowed or divorced are far more likely to be over 50 than are persons who have never married, most of whom are young adults who soon will marry. So our diagram is an accurate summary of the relationships.

These results are unusually clean. Typically, when control variables are used, there will be some "bounce," or random fluctuation, in the subtables because of the small numbers of cases in some columns. We can see more of the messiness of real analysis in the following example of an intervening variable.

Social scientists have noted that some individuals move because they are "pushed" by lack of opportunities in their current location, while others move because they are "pulled" by the attraction of opportunity elsewhere; this is called the "push/pull" hypothesis of geographic mobility. This hypothesis suggests that individuals who have moved since they were 16 would be likely to have higher incomes than those who didn't move. Return to the beginning of the **Tabular Statistics** task and *select* **23** or **INCOME** as the row variable and **11** or **MOVERS** as the column variable. Use column percentaging.

```
Row Variable: 23) INCOME     Column Variable: 11) MOVERS

                     STAYER         MOVER
UNDER 15K             28.8           22.6
15K-29999K            26.3           23.2
30K & OVER            44.9           54.2

N                      597            869
```

Because this table has three rows, it is a little more difficult to read. Looking at the first row, we can see that stayers are slightly more likely than movers to have incomes under $15,000. Look at the bottom row; movers are more likely than stayers to have incomes over $30,000. Movers generally have higher incomes than stayers. (If you prefer, you can read the table by looking at the first row: 28.8 percent of the stayers have incomes under $15,000 compared with 22.6 percent of the movers. Then you can add the first two rows together: 55.1 percent of the stayers have incomes less than $30,000 compared with 45.8 percent of the movers. Stayers generally have lower incomes than movers.)

We might speculate that educational attainment is an intervening variable: Individuals move to get more education, and higher educational attainment leads to higher-paying jobs. We can diagram this argument:

Notice that, when we are dealing with intervening variables, the variable comes between the other two variables in time. Again the arrows represent causal relationships. We have argued that educational attainment is an intervening variable between moving and income, so, in this situation, we expect the relationship between moving and income to disappear when we control for educational attainment. Let's check this idea.

Return to the beginning of the task. *Select* **23** or **INCOME** as the row variable, **11** or **MOVERS** as the column variable, and **15** or **DEGREE** as the control variable. Do not select a second control variable and do not subset. The table for those with less than a high school degree appears first. Use column percentaging.

```
Control Category: NOT HI SCH
Row Variable: 23) INCOME     Column Variable: 11) MOVERS

                     STAYER         MOVER
    UNDER 15K         57.5           58.5
    15K-29999K        21.6           26.2
    30K & OVER        20.9           15.4

    N                 134            130
```

These differences are in the reverse direction from the original table. Movers are slightly more likely than stayers to have low incomes. You might note the N's for the columns are not large. *Press <ENTER> once* to view the table for high school graduates. Again, use column percentaging.

```
Control Category: HIGH SCH
Row Variable: 23 INCOME      Column Variable: 11 MOVERS

                        STAYER          MOVER
UNDER 15K               26.0            21.1
15K-29999K              30.7            28.8
30K & OVER              43.3            50.1

N                        335             427
```

Among high school graduates, the movers are likely to have higher incomes, but the effect is smaller than that in the original table. *Press <ENTER> to view the next table.* Use column percentaging.

```
Control Category: SOME COLL.
Row Variable: 23 INCOME      Column Variable: 11 MOVERS

                        STAYER          MOVER
UNDER 15K                6.3             9.3
15K-29999K              19.5            14.5
30K & OVER              74.2            76.2

N                        128             311
```

Among those with some college, movers are also likely to have higher incomes, but the effect is much weaker than in the original table.

Since the original relationship has been considerably weakened (and even reversed) in these subtables, our hypothesis has been supported; educational attainment may be an intervening variable between moving and income. When we controlled for the intervening variable, the relationship between the other two variables disappeared, or at least weakened. The diagram provides an accurate summary of the relationships.

Let's pause for a moment to summarize the difference between spurious and intervening relationships. To test for spuriousness, we control for a variable and examine the relationship between two variables. To test for an intervening variable, we do exactly the same thing. The only difference is the time order of the variables. With a spurious relationship, the control variable precedes the other two variables. With an intervening relationship, the control variable comes between the other two variables.

Let's look at another example of a three-variable relationship. We might reason that individuals with low family incomes are more likely to live in neighborhoods with high crime rates and, consequently, might be more worried about walking alone at night. Return to the beginning of the task. Use **13** or **FEAR WALK** as the row variable and **23** or **INCOME** as the column variable. Use column percentaging.

```
Row Variable: 13) FEAR WALK    Column Variable: 23) INCOME

                  UNDER 15K     15K-29999K     30K & OVER
     YES            50.4           45.9           38.3
     NO             49.6           54.1           61.7

     N              246            246            499
```

In fact, this appears to be the case.

Generally, crime is associated with cities. We might further think this fear is only a problem of urban residents, and that the relationship between fear of walking and income is a consequence of poor urban neighborhoods:

In this diagram, we have predicted that the relationship between income and fear of walking will disappear when we control for urbanity of neighborhood.

To test this idea, we would control for area of residence, 10) PLACE SIZE, and re-examine this relationship. So, repeat the previous analysis using **10** or **PLACE SIZE** as the control variable. You should be able to obtain each of the following tables (remember to use column percentaging).

```
Control category: CITY/SUBUR
Row Variable: 13) FEAR WALK    Column Variable: 23) INCOME

                  UNDER 15K     15K-29999K     30K & OVER
     YES            71.0           61.2           48.7
     NO             29.0           38.8           51.3

     N              69             85             265


Control category: SMALL CITY
Row Variable: 13) FEAR WALK    Column Variable: 23) INCOME

                  UNDER 15K     15K-29999K     30K & OVER
     YES            45.2           42.5           32.7
     NO             54.8           57.5           67.3

     N              115            106            153
```

```
Control category: TOWN/FARM
Row Variable: 13) FEAR WALK    Column Variable: 23) INCOME

                UNDER 15K      15K-29999K      30K & OVER
     YES          34.0           24.4           12.3
     NO           66.0           75.6           87.7

     N             47             41             65
```

Study each of these tables. We can see that area of residence does have a powerful effect; 71 percent of the lowest income group in urban areas reported fear of walking at night, while only 34 percent of this group were afraid in villages and in the country. However, the effect of income still persists, regardless of area of residence. Aside from some minor bounce, individuals with higher incomes reported less fear than individuals with lower incomes. So in this example, both variables have an effect on the dependent variable, and the diagram is not correct.

We could rediagram this result to reflect the observed relationships:

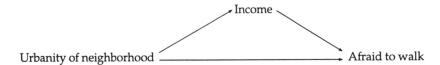

In this example, both independent variables have an effect on the dependent variable.

Your turn.

NAME: _____

COURSE: _____

DATE: _____

EXERCISE

5a

Workbook exercises and software are copyrighted. Copying is prohibited by law.

WORKSHEET

1. a. In the example showing that educational attainment is an intervening variable between moving and income, what time order of the variables was assumed? That is, which variable occurred first, which occurred second, and which occurred last?

   First: _____

   Second: _____

   Third: _____

   b. Suppose we had argued that people move *after* they have finished their education. Draw the appropriate diagram for this time order.

   c. Look again at the statistical results. How would this change in time order affect the interpretation of the relationships among these three variables?

2. *Open* the **SURVEY** data file.

   a. What is the description of variable **86) READ PAPER**?

      _____

      _____

   b. Go to the **STATISTICAL ANALYSIS** menu and *select* **Tabular Statistics**. Using **111** or **VISIT ART** as the row variable and **86** or **READ PAPER** as the column variable, use column percentaging to fill in the following table:

	DAILY	WEEKLY	SELDOM
YES	%	%	%
NO	%	%	%

What is the value of V? _____

Prob. = _____

Is this significant? (Circle one.)   Yes   No

Describe the relationship shown in this table.

   c. We might argue that this is a spurious relationship and that both of these variables are affected by educational attainment. Draw the diagram that would represent this argument.

   d. Now conduct the same analysis using **111** or **VISIT ART** as the row variable, **86** or **READ PAPER** as the column variable, and **15** or **DEGREE** as the control variable. Fill in each of the tables using column percentaging.

Control category: NOT HI SCH

	DAILY	WEEKLY	SELDOM
YES	%	%	%
NO	%	%	%

What is the value of V? _____

Prob. = _____

Is this significant? (Circle one.)   Yes   No

Control category: HIGH SCH

	DAILY	WEEKLY	SELDOM
YES	%	%	%
NO	%	%	%

What is the value of V? _____

Prob. = _____

Is this significant? (Circle one.)   Yes   No

Control category: SOME COLL.

	DAILY	WEEKLY	SELDOM
YES	%	%	%
NO	%	%	%

What is the value of V? _____

Prob. = _____

Is this significant? (Circle one.)   Yes   No

e. Draw a diagram summarizing the results.

f. How would you interpret these results?

3. a. Using **12** or **HUNT/FISH** as the row variable and **46** or **CH.ATTEND** as the column variable, use column percentaging to fill in the following table:

	NOT OFTEN	OFTEN
YES	%	%
NO	%	%

What is the value of V? _____

Prob. = _____

Is this significant? (Circle one.)   Yes   No

How would you interpret these results?

b. We might argue that this is a spurious relationship and that both of these variables are affected by gender: Women are more likely to go to church, and women are less likely to hunt. Draw the diagram that would represent this argument.

Conduct the same analysis using **1** or **SEX** as the control variable.

c. Control category: MALE

	NOT OFTEN	OFTEN
YES	%	%
NO	%	%

What is the value of V? _____

Prob. = _____

Is this significant? (Circle one.)   Yes   No

Control category: FEMALE

	NOT OFTEN	OFTEN
YES	%	%
NO	%	%

What is the value of V? _____

Prob. = _____

Is this significant? (Circle one.)   Yes   No

d. Draw a diagram summarizing the results.

e. How would you interpret these results?

4. a. Look at the description of each of these variables: **25) OWN HOME?, 24) $ 50%50%**, and **15) DEGREE**. Draw the diagram that would show **24) $ 50%50%** as an intervening variable between **15) DEGREE** and **25) OWN HOME?**.

   b. To test this model, which variable should be used as the control variable? (Circle one.)

               25) OWN HOME?

               24) $ 50%50%

               15) DEGREE

   c. Use **Tabular Analysis** to test the hypothesis that **24) $ 50%50%** is an intervening variable between **15) DEGREE** and **25) OWN HOME?**. Label the two tables below and fill in the column percentages. Show Cramer's V and decide whether the relationships are statistically significant.

Control Category: _____

_____			
_____			
_____			

What is the value of V? _____

Prob. = _____

Is this significant? (Circle one.)   Yes   No

Control Category: _____

_____			
_____			
_____			

What is the value of V? _____

Prob. = _____

Is this significant? (Circle one.)   Yes   No

d. What is your interpretation of the results?

5. Let's use data from the **SURVEY** data file to test the following causal hypothesis: Veterans are less afraid to walk at night than are non-veterans.

a. What is the description of **148) VETERAN?**

   _____

   _____

b. Use **13** or **FEAR WALK** as the row variable and **148** or **VETERAN?** as the column variable. Use column percentages to fill in the following table.

	VETERAN	NON-VET
YES		
NO		

What is the value of V? _____

Prob. = _____

Is this significant? (Circle one.)   Yes   No

Do the results support or reject the hypothesis?
(Circle one.)   Support   Reject

c. Select a variable in the **SURVEY** data set that might be a source of spuriousness. What is the number and name of this variable?

   _____

d. In the space below, present the tables which allow you to test for spuriousness using this variable:

e. Draw the diagram that best represents these results.

f. Summarize your findings in a brief paragraph.

6. a. Using the **SURVEY** data set, we found that some respondents expressed some impatience and hostility during the interview. Let's see if we can gain some understanding of what other factors might affect this variable. Use **128** or **ATTITUDE?** as the row variable and **15** or **DEGREE** as the column variable. Use column percentages to fill in the following table.

	NOT HI SCH	HIGH SCH	SOME COLL.
FRIENDLY	%	%	%
COOPERATIV	%	%	%
IMPAT/HOST	%	%	%

V = _____

Prob. = _____

b. Does education appear to have an effect on degree of cooperation? If so, describe the relationship.

c. Perhaps education affects cooperation because individuals with lower educational attainment are more likely to fail to understand the questions. Perhaps degree of comprehension (127) COMPREHEND) is an intervening variable between educational attainment and cooperation. Show the diagram that would represent this argument.

d. Test this argument using cross-tabulation. Finish labeling the following tables (to indicate the categories of the control variable) and fill in the results.

Control Category: _____

	NOT HI SCH	HIGH SCH	SOME COLL.
FRIENDLY	%	%	%
COOPERATIV	%	%	%
IMPAT/HOST	%	%	%

V = _____

Prob. = _____

Control Category: _____

	NOT HI SCH	HIGH SCH	SOME COLL.
FRIENDLY	%	%	%
COOPERATIV	%	%	%
IMPAT/HOST	%	%	%

V = _____

Prob. = _____

Control Category: _____

	NOT HI SCH	HIGH SCH	SOME COLL.
FRIENDLY	%	%	%
COOPERATIV	%	%	%
IMPAT/HOST	%	%	%

V = _____

Prob. = _____

e. What is your interpretation of these results?

f. What practical implications does this result have for developing survey questions that will encourage cooperation?

5b

Causal Models

In the previous exercise, we saw how quickly cases can evaporate in cross-tabular analysis, making interpretations extremely difficult. This happens even when we work with collapsed variables. In this exercise, we'll look at another technique, regression analysis, that can be used for the same type of analysis. This technique uses statistical procedures to unravel the influence of different independent variables and does not have the problem of running out of cases.

Open the **SURVEY** data file and go to the **Regression** task. *Press* the **F3** key and *press* **S** (for Search). *Type* **SAT.** and *press* *<ENTER>*. The variable 150) SAT.HEALT! appears in a box on the screen. The exclamation point in the name indicates that this is an uncollapsed form of the variable and therefore preserves the maximum amount of variation. In regression analysis, the more variation, the better. *Press* the **right arrow** to see the information on this variable. Notice that, although this variable has seven categories ranked from least to greatest satisfaction with one's health, this is not an interval variable but only an ordinal variable. Ideally, we use interval or ratio variables with regression, but we'll assume that this variable is close enough to an interval variable to be acceptable. *Select* **150** or **SAT.HEALT!** as the dependent variable and **133** or **AGE!** as the independent variable. *Press* *<ENTER>* in response to the next prompt and do not select a subset. The following regression graphic appears:

$$R\text{-}SQ = 0.01$$

$$133)\ AGE! \quad \underline{\quad\quad \underset{(r = -0.11)}{BETA = -0.11^{**}} \quad\quad} \quad 150)\ SAT.HEALT!$$

We can see that age seems to have some effect on an individual's satisfaction with his or her health; looking at the value of R^2, we can see that age explains 1 percent of the variation in satisfaction with health (what appears on the screen is the proportion of variance explained; to convert it into a percentage, simply move the decimal point two places to the right). The effect of age is significant at the .01 level as the beta is followed by two asterisks.

It seems quite likely that older individuals are in worse actual health than younger individuals. Consequently, it could be that the actual health of the individual is an intervening variable linking age and satisfaction with one's health. Variable 149) HEALTH! is an ordinal variable measuring current health. *Press <ENTER> to return to the beginning of the task. Select* **150** or **SAT.HEALT!** as the dependent variable, **133** or **AGE!** as the first independent variable, and **149** or **HEALTH!** as the second and final independent variable. Do not select a subset. The following graphic will appear:

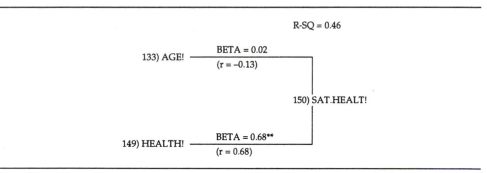

The correlation coefficient of each independent variable with the dependent variable is shown below each line. We can see that actual health (as perceived by the respondent) has an extremely large correlation with satisfaction with health: r = 0.68. When this is combined with age, 46 percent of the variation (see R^2) in satisfaction is explained.

The beta values indicate the effect of one independent variable when the effects of the other independent variables have been controlled. If we look at the beta for the effect of age (.02), we can see its effect has disappeared—even turning slightly in the reverse direction. The effect of actual health on satisfaction with health is virtually unchanged when we control for age (.68).

This diagram differs from those in the previous exercise. Regression focuses on variation in the dependent variable and ignores relationships among the independent variables. Consequently, neither the time order of the two independent variables nor the relationship between them is represented in the diagram. We could show these same results using our previous diagram:

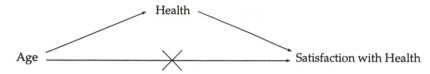

Press **A** (for Anova) to see the same information in a tabular form:

```
DEPENDENT VAR. 150) SAT.HEALT!
N: 521    Missing: 1,085
MULTIPLE R-SQUARE = 0.46  Y-INTERCEPT = 1.54

SOURCE          Sum of Squares     DF      Mean Square
REGRESSION         579.48          2         289.74
RESIDUAL           684.78         518          1.32
TOTAL             1264.26         520

F = 219.17
Prob. = 0.000

                Unstand.b    Stand.Beta    Std.Err.b        t
133) AGE!         0.00         0.02          0.00          0.70
149) HEALTH!      1.25         0.68          0.06         20.52**
```

Focus only on the information that is shown above in bold. Notice that the number of cases used in this analysis is only 521; all other cases had missing data on one or more of these variables. We can see that the effect of the two variables combined is statistically significant (Prob. = 0.000). The effect of 149) HEALTH! is significant at the .01 level; the t statistic is followed by two asterisks. The effect of 133) AGE! is no longer significant; the t statistic has no asterisks.

These results tell us that health is indeed an intervening variable between age and satisfaction with health. The effect of age on satisfaction disappeared when we controlled for actual health. That is, older people are as satisfied with their health as are younger people so long as both have good health or both have poor health. Health is the link. Again the interpretation hinges on our assumption about the time order of the variables. If we had assumed that health preceded age, then we would have concluded that the relationship between age and satisfaction with health was spurious.

In Exercise 5a, we looked at the effect of moving and education on income. Educational attainment appeared to be an intervening variable between moving and income. Let's look at this same example, using regression analysis. First, we should note that 11) MOVERS is not an ordinal variable; it is a nominal variable with two categories, zero for stayers and one for movers. This is a *dummy* variable and can be used as an *independent* variable in regression analysis. Instead of using collapsed versions of the other variables as we did when we used tabular analysis, we'll use 137) INCOME! as our measure of income and 135) EDUCATION! as our measure of education.

Select **137** or **INCOME!** as the dependent variable. *Select* **11** or **MOVERS** as the first independent variable and **135** or **EDUCATION!** as the second independent variable. Do not select a subset. The following graphic will appear:

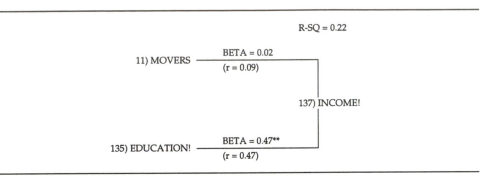

The effect of moving on income has essentially been removed by controlling for education. So again we can conclude that education is an intervening variable.

Now let's try this regression task with aggregate data. *Open* the **USA** data file and again *select* the **Regression** task. In Exercise 2a, we looked at the relationship between hunting and the murder rate and found a significant negative relationship. Murder is an interactive crime that almost always involves contact between the victim and the murderer. This would suggest that murder rates should increase when the amount of contact between individuals increases. For example, during summer months when the weather is pleasant, people spend more time outside and have more contact with one another. In fact, the murder rate is higher in summer than in winter. Areas also differ in their winter weather; in some states, winter is just as pleasant as summer. These states should have higher murder rates than states with extremely cold winters.

Select **109** or **MURDER** as the dependent variable, **72** or **HUNTING** as the first independent variable, and **37** or **WARM WINTR** as the second independent variable:

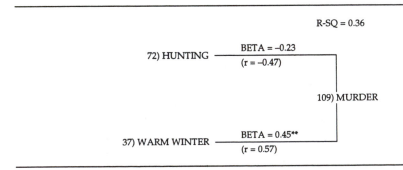

The temperature in winter has a strong relationship with the murder rate: r = 0.57. *Press* **A** (for Anova) to see the analysis of variance table. The effect of hunting is no longer significant. Controlling for weather caused a big drop in the effect of hunting on the murder rate. This suggests that the original negative relationship was spurious.

Your turn.

NAME: _____

COURSE: _____

DATE: _____

EXERCISE

5b

WORKSHEET

1. *Open* the **SURVEY** data file. Test the following causal argument using regression analysis: "The higher their incomes, the more likely people are to support freedom of speech. However, this is really a spurious relationship, since both variables are the result of education—education increases both income and toleration of unpopular speech."

    Diagram this argument using **135) EDUCATION!**, **138) R.INCOME!**, and **85) FREE SPEAK**.

    Use regression analysis to test this causal interpretation. *Press* **P** to print the regression graphic in MicroCase. (NOTE: If your computer is not connected to a printer or if you have been instructed not to use the printer, just skip these printing instructions.)

    a. What is the dependent variable?_____

    b. List the independent variables and provide the value of standard beta and the level of significance for each variable.

VARIABLE NAME	STANDARD BETA	SIGNIFICANCE (Circle one.)	
_____	_____	Yes	No
_____	_____	Yes	No

    c. What is the value of the multiple R^2? _____

    d. What is the level of significance of R^2? _____

e. Is the causal argument that education is the antecedent variable and the source of a spurious relationship supported or rejected? (Circle one.)   Supported   Rejected

f. Cite the evidence which supports this conclusion.

2. Test the following causal argument using regression analysis: "Both father's and mother's education influence how much education their children get."

Diagram this argument using 20) DAD EDUC!, 21) MOM EDUC!, and 135) EDUCATION!.

Use regression analysis to test this causal interpretation. *Press* **P** to print the regression graphic in MicroCase.

a. What is the dependent variable?   _____

b. List the independent variables and provide the value of standard beta and the level of significance for each variable.

VARIABLE NAME	STANDARD BETA	SIGNIFICANCE (Circle one.)	
_____	_____	Yes	No
_____	_____	Yes	No

c. What is the value of the multiple R^2?   _____

d. What is the level of significance of R^2? _____

e. Is the causal argument that the education of both
   parents causes the education of their offspring—
   that each plays an independent causal role—
   supported or rejected? (Circle one.) Supported Rejected

f. Cite the evidence which supports this conclusion.

3. Now use **143** or **PRAY!** as the dependent variable, **133** or **AGE!** as the first
   independent variable, and **1** or **SEX** as the second independent variable.
   Diagram the causal form you think these variables would fit.

Use regression analysis to test this causal interpretation. *Press* **P** to print the
regression graphic in MicroCase.

a. List the independent variables and provide the value of standard beta
   and the level of significance for each variable.

VARIABLE NAME	STANDARD BETA	SIGNIFICANCE (Circle one.)	
_____	_____	Yes	No
_____	_____	Yes	No

b. What is the value of the multiple R^2? _____

c. What is the level of significance of R^2? _____

d. Interpret these findings.

4. Test the following causal argument using regression analysis: "Father's edu-
    cation is strongly correlated with a respondent's income. The link between
    these two variables is the respondent's education. That is, the child's educa-
    tion is a crucial intervening variable by which affluence is passed from one
    generation to the next."

    Diagram this argument.

    Use regression analysis to test this causal interpretation. (Hints: Use the
    search feature to find the variables you need. In selecting your variables, use
    uncollapsed variables—variables that have an ! on the end of their names—
    and think in terms of *individual* income rather than family income.) Print the
    resulting graphic in MicroCase.

    a. What is the dependent variable?   _____

    b. In the following matrix, list the independent variables and provide the
       value of standard beta and the level of significance for each variable.

       VARIABLE NAME   STANDARD BETA   SIGNIFICANCE (Circle one.)

       _____   _____   Yes   No

       _____   _____   Yes   No

    c. What is the value of the multiple R²?   _____

    d. What is the level of significance of R^2?   _____

    e. Is the causal argument that the respondent's education is the intervening variable supported or rejected? (Circle one.)   Supported   Rejected

    f. Explain your answer, citing the most relevant results.

5. *Open* the **USA** data file. Look at the effect of **81) $ PER CAP.** and **90) % COLLEGE** on **100) BOOK $**. Diagram what you believe to be the causal connections among these variables.

    a. What is the dependent variable?   _____

    b. List the independent variables and provide the value of standard beta and the level of significance for each variable.

VARIABLE NAME	STANDARD BETA	SIGNIFICANCE (Circle one.)
_____	_____	Yes No
_____	_____	Yes No

    c. What is the value of the multiple R^2? _____

    d. What is the level of significance of R^2? _____

    e. How would you interpret these results?

6. Look at the effect of **58) PLAYBOY** and **27) MALE HOMES** on **46) ALCO-HOL**.

   a. What is the dependent variable? _____

   b. What is the value of r (shown below the line in the graphic) between **PLAYBOY** and **ALCOHOL**? _____

   c. What is the value of r between **MALE HOMES** and **ALCOHOL**? _____

   d. List the independent variables and provide the value of standard beta and the level of significance for each variable.

VARIABLE NAME	STANDARD BETA	SIGNIFICANCE (Circle one.)	
_____	_____	Yes	No
_____	_____	Yes	No

   e. What is the value of the multiple R^2? _____

   f. What is its level of significance? _____

   g. How would you interpret these results?

Selecting a Study Design

OVERVIEW

Different kinds of research questions require different types of research designs. Each type of research (experiments, field studies, surveys, etc.) has advantages and disadvantages. In this exercise, you will gain experience in selecting the appropriate type of research in order to answer a particular type of research question.

BEFORE YOU BEGIN

Please make sure you have read Chapter 6 in the textbook and can answer the following review questions (you need not write any answers):

1. Describe the two fundamental features of experiments.

2. Explain why the experiment is the most powerful research design.

3. Give two reasons social scientists cannot always use experiments.

4. What is the big advantage of survey research and what is its chief disadvantage?

5. What is field research and in what situations is it most useful?

6. What is aggregate or comparative research and how are data collected for such research?

7. Describe the general purpose of content analysis.

The text identifies the following types of research: survey research, comparative research, field research, experimental research, and content analysis. These categories reflect the way in which studies are generally described by social scientists: "Her experiment showed . . . ," "He used content analysis to test the idea that . . . ," "Our survey results suggest that . . . ," and so on. Classifying studies in this way identifies the type of research by its most salient element. Survey research, for example, emphasizes a data collection technique, while content analysis is basically a measurement technique, developing measures by coding content. This is a loose categorization and allows us to examine the elements that are usually combined in each design. In this exercise, we'll look at the types of research questions that are best suited to each design.

These designs differ in the degree of structure required in the research question. Experimental research requires a highly structured question, since the manipulation of the independent variable is built into the actual design of the study. Field research requires the least structured question since the researcher is able to observe anything of interest. The other approaches tend to fall between these two extremes. The formulation of the research question then is one of the first considerations in selecting a design.

In *exploratory* research, the research question is usually unstructured. Researchers are typically interested in a particular phenomenon and are still searching for connections with other phenomena. *Field* research is frequently used in this situation. For example, a researcher interested in how a new member is socialized into a deviant group might well start by observing how members of such a group interact with a new member or a potential member. When a research question is phrased using "how," field research is probably the best approach. Based on these observations, the researcher might develop some hypotheses on "why" certain approaches are more successful than others or "why" some members are more easily socialized than others.

When a researcher is interested in causes, or why certain phenomena happen, other designs are more appropriate. An *experiment* is the most powerful method for testing a causal hypothesis, since the problem of spuriousness is eliminated in the design of the study. So, when testing causal hypotheses, the researcher should first evaluate the possibility of conducting an experiment. Is the independent concept subject to manipulation? Can subjects be assigned randomly to levels of the independent variable? If the independent concept *can* be manipulated and subjects *can* be randomly assigned to levels of the independent variable, then the use of an experiment should be considered. In evaluating social programs, for example, subjects frequently can be assigned to different "treatments," and experimental research is a viable option. Incidentally, while most experiments use individuals as the unit of analysis, other units can be used. For example, a company selling to small businesses might use an experiment to compare the effectiveness of two different marketing approaches. In this study, small businesses would be the unit of analysis and each business would be assigned randomly to one of the two marketing approaches.

Two additional concerns should be addressed before deciding to use an experimental design: ethical questions and feasibility questions. Even if it is possible to manipulate the independent concept, it may not be ethical to do so. For example, one could use an experiment to assess the relative effectiveness of spanking in eliminating undesirable behaviors in children, but randomly assigning children to experimental treatments, one of which involved spanking, raises serious ethical questions. Even when the manipulation of the independent variable raises no ethical concerns, it may not be feasible to conduct an experiment. For example, one could test the effectiveness of a suicide-prevention education program by using an experiment: High school students could be randomly assigned to participate in the program or not. However, this study would not be feasible. Because suicide is a rare phenomenon and very few subjects in either treatment condition would ever commit suicide, an enormous number of subjects would be required to reliably compare the suicide rate across experimental conditions.

If an experiment cannot be used, naturally occurring variation of the independent concept must be measured. With the remaining three designs (survey research, comparative research, and content analysis), the logic of testing causal hypotheses is the same. With each, one must not only examine the relationship between the independent and dependent concepts, but also consider potential sources of spuriousness. So the choice of design hinges on the unit of analysis used in the research question and the nature of the concepts.

If the unit used in the research question is an aggregation, then the best test of the hypothesis would be with data on the relevant unit. With most aggregate units, the researcher can use only data that already has been collected—it wouldn't really be feasible to collect data to determine the gross domestic product of each of a set of nations. Lack of appropriate data is frequently a problem in comparative research. With some aggregate units, surveys of "key" persons can be used to supplement existing data. For example, research questions about cities might be addressed by surveying mayors of an appropriate sample of cities. In some cases, it might be possible to use content analysis to create appropriate measures. For example, if you were interested in the effect of legal codes on various types of crime, you might be able to use content analysis of written legal codes to create the independent variable. Or with the Human Area Relations Files, you could use content analysis to code characteristics of societies from field notes recorded by anthropologists.

If the unit of analysis is an individual, then survey research is probably the most appropriate design. Except for ethical issues, the only limits on survey research are that you must be able to identify the appropriate population, to select a sample from this population, if necessary, and to collect information on the relevant concepts by asking questions.

Study designs are not mutually exclusive—elements of two or more may be incorporated into the same study. For example, in the experiment described in the text, subjects are shown information about a political candidate in which gender is the independent variable. Information on the dependent variable, candidate preference, could be collected in a variety of ways. The subjects might be asked to cast a single vote. Or they could be asked to fill out a questionnaire. Or they might be asked to write an essay on the relative merits of the candidates. Content analysis of the essay might be used to develop a measure of the dependent variable.

There are many other ways in which elements of more than one technique might be combined in a single study. A field researcher might survey the members of a group being observed. Or a survey study might have interviewers code information about an individual's living room—a bit of field research. Studies evaluating social programs frequently employ "field experiments"—randomly assigning subjects to one of several experimental treatments conducted in natural settings.

In designing research, the most important task is to examine the research question and to collect data in the manner most appropriate for answering this question.

NAME: _____

COURSE: _____

DATE: _____

EXERCISE

6

WORKSHEET

1. For each of the following research questions, circle **YES** or **NO** to indicate whether it is possible to use an experiment to answer the research question. If it is not possible to use an experiment, explain why. If an experiment is possible, describe any ethical issue or feasibility problem that might prohibit experimentation.

a. Do college admissions committees discriminate on the basis of race?

NO (Explain below)

YES (Describe below any ethical issue or feasibility problem)

b. Is *Time* magazine more favorable to Democrats than to Republicans?

NO (Explain below)

YES (Describe below any ethical issue or feasibility problem)

c. Are women more religious than men?

NO (Explain below)

YES (Describe below any ethical issue or feasibility problem)

d. Are people who own cats less likely than those who own dogs to buy four-wheel-drive vehicles?

NO (Explain below)

YES (Describe below any ethical issue or feasibility problem)

e. Will people's judgments about art be more influenced by the opinions of their friends than by the opinions of strangers?

NO (Explain below)

YES (Describe below any ethical issue or feasibility problem)

f. When election ballots list candidates alphabetically, does this give an advantage to people whose names start with letters that come early in the alphabet?

NO (Explain below)

YES (Describe below any ethical issue or feasibility problem)

2. For each of the following research questions, circle the design (experimental, survey, comparative, field, or content analysis) that you think is best and explain why.

a. Are people who live in interracial neighborhoods less racially prejudiced than those who don't? (Circle one.)

Experimental   Survey   Comparative   Field   Content Analysis

Explain:

b. Do public television documentaries display a liberal bias? (Circle one.)

Experimental   Survey   Comparative   Field   Content Analysis

Explain:

c. Do employers discriminate against short male applicants, preferring to hire tall men? (Circle one.)

Experimental   Survey   Comparative   Field   Content Analysis

Explain:

d. Do students get better grades the closer they sit to the front of the classroom? (Circle one.)

Experimental   Survey   Comparative   Field   Content Analysis

Explain:

e. Are people who listen to radio talk shows more conservative than those who don't? (Circle one.)

Experimental   Survey   Comparative   Field   Content Analysis

Explain:

f. What kinds of people stop and give money to people who stand at the curb with a sign saying they are homeless? (Circle one.)

Experimental   Survey   Comparative   Field   Content Analysis

Explain:

g. Are men or women more apt to believe in astrology? (Circle one.)

Experimental   Survey   Comparative   Field   Content Analysis

Explain:

3. Different kinds of research questions require different kinds of units of analysis (cases). For example, if you want to explain why some people are more supportive of democratic principles than others are, then you would use individuals as the units of analysis. For each of the following research questions, write in the blank space the unit of analysis for which you would need to collect data.

    a. To what extent are people's attitudes on political issues related to their demographic characteristics such as education or age?

    _____

    b. How is the unemployment rate in cities related to the percentage of a city's labor force engaged in manufacturing?

    _____

    c. Do increases in economic development within nations lead to smaller family sizes?

    _____

    d. What kinds of newspapers are most likely to endorse Democratic candidates for public office?

    _____

    e. What kinds of social, economic, and political values are reflected in prime-time dramas on television?

    _____

    f. Does the size of a police department have an effect on how responsive it is to citizen complaints?

    _____

g. Do bars tend to specialize? That is, do different bars attract different kinds of regular customers?

_____

h. Why are some families more likely to do things together than others are?

_____

4. For some research designs, it is very important to consider change over time. For each of the following research questions, circle **Yes** or **No** to indicate whether the research would need to use data from at least two different time periods.

a. Are there differences in the political attitudes of men and women? (Circle one.)   Yes   No

b. If there is a "gender gap" in the political attitudes of men and women, is this gap getting bigger or smaller? (Circle one.)   Yes   No

c. Is the average family size smaller in more urbanized nations than it is in less urbanized nations? (Circle one.)   Yes   No

d. As nations become more urbanized, does the average family size decrease? (Circle one.)   Yes   No

e. Can a television documentary on drug use change attitudes? (Circle one.)   Yes   No

f. Are there regional differences in attitudes toward racial integration? (Circle one.)   Yes   No

g. Have attitudes about sexual behavior changed since the advent of AIDS? (Circle one.)   Yes   No

h. Do members of the American Communist Party hold different views now than they did before the breakup of the Soviet Union? (Circle one.)   Yes   No

5. Sometimes, we need to combine more than one method in order to investigate research questions. For each of the following situations, circle the *two* methods that we would probably need to use and provide a brief description of how they would be combined.

    a. Are there liberal-conservative differences among news magazines (*Time, Newsweek*, etc.), and are these differences reflected in the views of their readers? (Circle one.)

        Experimental   Survey   Comparative   Field   Content Analysis

        Briefly describe how you would combine these methods.

    b. Do the "messages" of restroom-wall graffiti vary according to the type of social environment in which the restroom exists? (Circle one.)

        Experimental   Survey   Comparative   Field   Content Analysis

        Briefly describe how you would combine these methods.

    c. Are people who display flags outside their houses on the Fourth of July more supportive of basic democratic principles than are those who do not display flags? (Circle one.)

        Experimental   Survey   Comparative   Field   Content Analysis

        Briefly describe how you would combine these methods.

7

Survey Analysis

OVERVIEW

In this exercise, you will learn about entering survey data into a computer data file, checking for errors, deciding which responses (e.g., "don't know") to treat as missing, and collapsing variables into a smaller set of categories to make them more convenient for certain types of analysis. You also will gain experience in identifying problems in the wording of survey questions and will take a closer look at contingency questions.

BEFORE YOU BEGIN

Please make sure you have read Chapter 7 in the textbook and can answer the following review questions (you need not write any answers):

1. What three main factors cause reliability problems in survey research?

2. Compare the advantages/disadvantages of interviews and questionnaires.

3. Compare the advantages/disadvantages of telephone and face-to-face interviews.

4. What are the benefits of using standard questions in surveys?

5. Compare the advantages/disadvantages of closed and open-ended questions.

6. What problems (e.g., bias) should be considered in writing survey questions?

7. Why are forced option questions better than cafeteria questions?

8. What is a contingency question?

9. In terms of response bias among survey respondents, what are the problems of conformity and response set?

10. How is a trend study different from a panel or longitudinal study?

11. Describe the differences among age, cohort, and period effects.

12. What ethical concerns are particularly relevant to survey research?

How to ask questions that respondents can and will answer is the primary challenge in conducting survey research. The text provides considerable guidance in avoiding various problems in question construction—you'll get a chance to evaluate the quality of various questions in the written exercises. However, even after the data have been collected, there is still a great deal of work to do before you can analyze the data.

After the surveys have been administered, the responses from the printed forms must be converted to electronic data. Let's see how this process works with MicroCase. Start MicroCase and *open* the file named **TEST**. This data file already has variables defined for the following mini-survey:

1. What is your present year in college?
    1. First
    2. Second
    3. Third
    4. Fourth
    5. Fifth or more

2. Do you live at home, in a dorm, or where?
    1. At home with my parent(s)
    2. In my own apartment or house
    3. In a dorm
    4. In a sorority
    5. In a fraternity

3. During an average week, how many hours do you spend studying for college?_____ (write in number)

On the **DATA AND FILE MANAGEMENT** menu, *select* **C. Enter Data from Keyboard**. You have three format options for entering data. *Type* **2** and *press* *<ENTER>* to select data entry by column. You will be entering new data so *press* *<ENTER>* to accept the first option provided to you. *Type* **1** and *press* *<ENTER>* to indicate that you will be entering data for the first case. In response to the next prompt, just *press* *<ENTER>* to enter data for all three variables. If everything is correct, *press* *<ENTER>* at the next prompt.

Let's assume the first respondent answered, "Third," to the first question (year in college). As you can see above, this is coded as a 3. So *type* **3** and *press* *<ENTER>*. For the second question (place of residence), *type* **6** and *press* *<ENTER>*. This is not a legitimate value—MicroCase warns you that the value is outside the range specified for the variable. *Press* *<ENTER>* to close this warning window. Suppose the respondent refused to answer this question. Replace the **6** with a blank and *press* *<ENTER>*. The computer again beeps to warn you that this is not one of the standard codes, but it will accept the blank. Although the value does not immediately appear on the screen as such, the computer will store the missing data code of –9999 as the value for this question. *Type* **24** and *press* <*ENTER*> for the answer to the third question (hours of studying).

Even though each answer is checked to make sure that the range is correct and you are warned by a beep when a question is left blank, data entry mistakes are easy to make. To guarantee accuracy, a technique called *rekey verification* is frequently used. With this technique, the data are entered twice. First, the data are entered using any of the data entry options. Then, the data are entered a second time using "rekey verification." This checking technique is based on the assumption that a data entry error is unlikely to occur a second time on the same response. You may remember that this is the same basic idea used to construct measures of reliability. By rekeying the data, we increase the reliability of the data. Let's see how this works.

Select the **Enter Data from Keyboard** task. Again *type* **2** and *press* <*ENTER*> to select data entry by column. Now *type* **3** and *press* <*ENTER*> to select the rekey verification option. Again select to enter data for the first case on all variables—*type* **1** and *press* <*ENTER*> *three times*. The screen appears exactly as it did before. *Type* **2** and *press* <*ENTER*>. The following warning appears:

```
Old Value: 3
New Value: 2
O) Old value or N) New value
```

This value does not match the previously entered value of 3. At this point, you must decide which is the correct response. *Type* **O** (for Old value). Enter the same values as before for the remaining variables.

Obviously, an enormous amount of work can be saved if the responses are entered directly into an electronic file. Computer Assisted Telephone Interview (CATI) and Computer Assisted Personal Interview (CAPI) systems have been developed to allow researchers to use computers for administering questionnaires. Each question appears on the screen. The respondent, or an interviewer, marks the appropriate response and the interview moves to the next question. As the use of personal computers and on-line communications increases, the use of such systems is also likely to increase.

Let's see how the CATI system works in MicroCase. *Open* the data file named **CATI**. From the **DATA AND FILE MANAGEMENT** menu, *select* **C. Enter Data from Keyboard**. Because of the way this data file was originally created, there is an additional data entry option available called "with template." *Type* **4** and *press* <*ENTER*> to select data entry with template. *Type* **1** and *press* <*ENTER*> to enter new data. *Press* <*ENTER*> in response to the next prompt. *Type* **1** and *press* <*ENTER*> to enter data for the first case. *Press* <*ENTER*> to continue. *Press* <*ENTER*> to begin the interview. The first question appears and the possible answers are shown in the box at the bottom. A check mark appears next to the bottom category. To select an answer, either you may move the check mark to the appropriate response and press <ENTER> or you may type the number of the response and press <ENTER>. *Use either of these methods to select your answer.* You are now moved to the next question. You are moved through the questionnaire in this manner until you reach the end. If you wish to go back to an earlier question, *press* the **<Ctrl>** and **<Page Up>** keys *together.* Go ahead and answer questions 1 through 5 any way you like to see how this works. (Stop when you come to the question asking marital status.)

There are two main advantages of using such systems. First, the data are entered directly into the computer—answers do not have to be keyed into the computer from questionnaires. Second, complicated contingency questions can be preprogrammed. Let's look at an example of a contingency question.

The following set of questions was used in the 1990 General Social Survey to ascertain marital status:

16. Are you currently married, widowed, divorced, separated, or have you never been married?
Married (ASK A, B & D) 1
Widowed (ASK A & B) 2
Divorced (ASK A, C & D) 3
Separated (ASK A, C & D) 4
Never married (GO TO Q.17) 5

IF EVER MARRIED:

A. How old were you when you first married?

ENTER EXACT AGE

ASK ONLY IF CURRENTLY MARRIED OR WIDOWED:

B. Have you ever been divorced or legally separated?
Yes (ASK [1]) 1
No (GO TO INSTRUCTIONS
BEFORE D) 2

IF YES TO B:

[1] Did you obtain a divorce or separation during the past 12 months, that is, since (February/March) 1989?
Yes (ASK [2]) 1
No (ASK [2]) 2

[2] Did you (also) obtain a divorce or separation during the period 1985 through (February/March) 1989?
Yes (GO TO INSTRUCTIONS
BEFORE D) 1
No (GO TO INSTRUCTIONS
BEFORE D) 2

C. IF DIVORCED OR SEPARATED:

[1] Did you obtain a divorce or separation during the past 12 months, that is, since (February/March) 1989?
Yes (ASK [2]) 1
No (ASK [2]) 2

[2] Did you (also) obtain a divorce or separation during the period 1985 through (February/March) 1989?

       Yes (ASK D) 1

       No (ASK D). 2

IF CURRENTLY WIDOWED, SKIP TO Q.17; IF CURRENTLY MARRIED, SEPARATED, OR DIVORCED, ASK D.

D. Have you ever been widowed?

       Yes 1

       No. 2

Notice that interviewers are to ask certain questions, called contingency questions, only if previous questions are answered in particular ways. Look at the beginning of question 16. If the respondent answers, "Divorced," then the interviewer is to ask parts A, C, and D. If the respondent is married, then questions A, B, and D are to be asked. The answer to question B determines whether part B[2] is asked, and so on. Sometimes, the branching procedures can be even more complicated. In some cases, the questions may be separated by several pages. For example, in this survey, question 23 (a question about spouse's employment status) was to be asked only of those who indicated on question 16 that they were currently married. You can see why interviewers need to be carefully trained. On self-administered questionnaires, contingency questions must be quite simple or the respondent will get lost.

Continue to the sixth question on the computer. Questions 6 through 11 are exactly the same questions used in the General Social Survey shown above. *Select* **response 5**—you are asked no additional questions about marital status. Now *press* <Ctrl> and <Page Up> to go back to the sixth question. This time, *select* **response 3**, Divorced. Now you are asked additional questions about marital status. The exact set of questions depends on the responses to these additional questions. If you go back to the sixth question and change your answer, you will be sent through another question path. Go ahead and answer the remaining questions in this survey any way you like. When you answer the final question, you will be returned to the main menu in MicroCase.

The flow of questions is controlled by a series of instructions—in MicroCase, these instructions are called a *data entry template*. While the student version of MicroCase does not allow you to do so, creating templates is an easy process. Extremely complicated contingencies can be handled using templates of this type. So CATI/CAPI systems not only allow direct data entry into an electronic format, but also allow complete control over the flow of the questionnaire.

Even after the data are in electronic form, there is still work to be done to prepare the data for analysis. Not all respondents take surveys seriously, and some may intentionally give inappropriate responses. There are several ways to check for such responses. When the values of a variable are not limited to particular categories, you should look at the univariate distribution to see if there are any extreme values. For example, in one year of the GSS, one individual claimed a lifetime total of 403 female sexual partners. This seemed highly unlikely when compared to the rest of the sample. But closer examination of this case revealed that the respondent was a 69-year-old man who reported having 5 to 10 sexual partners during the previous 12 months. He claimed casual pickups and paid sexual partners in addition to his wife. Assuming this man had been similarly active since the age of 20, his claim of 403 partners over his lifetime seems reasonable, even if the precision of the answer seems rather startling.

Another way to check for inappropriate responses is to examine the associations between variables known to have certain relationships. For example, in a college survey, students may be asked their sex and their place of residence. We know that anyone living in a fraternity should be male. If we find one or more females claiming to live in a fraternity, we probably would want to check their responses to other questions. In a high school survey, one student claimed to be 7 feet tall and weigh 100 pounds. This is highly unlikely.

What should you do if you identify a suspicious value? There are three options: Change that value to missing data, eliminate the case completely, or create a "flag" variable. To use a "flag" variable, you first create a new variable with the values 0 and 1 (or actually any values that you wish). If a case appears to have inappropriate data, you set the value of this flag variable to 1; otherwise, the case is given a value of 0. When you analyze the data, you always select a subset of those cases that have a 0 on this flag variable. The advantage of using a flag variable rather than eliminating cases is that the data still exist for other analyses or other researchers.

Another aspect of cleaning survey data for analysis involves answers such as "don't know" and "no answer." Generally, we want these answers to be treated as missing data during analysis. In MicroCase, the easiest method of doing this is to list these as additional categories of missing data. *Open* the **SURVEY** data file. *Go* to the **STATISTICAL ANALYSIS** menu and *select* the **Univariate Statistics** task. Obtain the distribution of **31) EVER STRAY**. Notice that 57 cases are in the category "NO ANSWER."

Press <ENTER> several times until you return to the beginning of the task. *Press* **F5**. *Type* **Y** and *press <ENTER>* in response to the prompt of whether you want to continue. You are asked for the list of category names to be treated as missing. *Type* **NO ANSWER** and *press <ENTER>*. *Press <ENTER> enough times* to close the window. Now look at the distribution of **31) EVER STRAY** again. Notice the category "NO ANSWER" has been dropped from the distribution. If you fail to eliminate such categories before analysis, relationships can be seriously distorted.

Frequently, you will want to analyze survey data using cross-tabulation techniques. As we saw in Exercise 5a, some variables must be "collapsed" before they can be used. MicroCase has a very easy method of combining categories of variables. Return to the **DATA AND FILE MANAGEMENT** menu. *Select* **B. Collapse/Strip Categories.** You are asked for the variable to be collapsed. *Type* **133** and *press <ENTER>. Press <ENTER> again* to accept 154 as the number for the new collapsed variable. You are asked for the name of the new collapsed variable, and the name of the uncollapsed variable is presented. *Delete* the name of the uncollapsed variable, *type* **AGE COL** as the name of the new collapsed variable, and *press <ENTER>.* The description of the variable to be collapsed is shown. *Press* **<End>** to go to the end of the description. *Type* **(collapsed)** at the end and *press <ENTER>.* You are now asked if you wish the distribution to be shown during the collapse. *Type* **1** to select the **with distribution** option and *press <ENTER>.*

The distribution of 133) AGE! is shown on the screen. The distribution of 154) AGE COL will be shown at the lower right as the variable is created. Information on the category directly above the arrow is shown at the lower left—there are five cases at age 18. We will create a new variable with five age categories: 18–29, 30–39, 40–49, 50–64, and 65 and over. *Press* **1** to place 18-year-olds in category 1. The arrow now moves to the next category. *Press* **1** to place 19-year-olds in category 1. *Continue pressing* **1** until you reach age 30 (do not assign 30 to this category). Now *press* **2** until you reach age 40. You can see the new variable being created at the lower right. You now have 302 cases in category 1 and 380 cases in category 2. This distribution is also shown graphically to the right in the form of a bar chart. *Press* **3** for ages 40 to 49, *press* **4** for ages 50 to 64, and *press* **5** for ages 65 to 89—age 89 actually already includes everyone ages 89 and up. If you need to make a correction to one of the categories, simply move the arrow to the incorrect category using the cursor keys and then assign the proper value. When you have finished, *press <ENTER>.*

The recode statement, which will be used for creating the new variable, is now shown. Just *press <ENTER>. Press <ENTER> again* to label the categories. Give the new categories the following labels: 18–29, 30–39, 40–49, 50–64, and 65 & OVER. *Press <ENTER>* after you name each category. When you have finished, *press <ENTER> again.* The new variable is now created. *Press <ENTER> again* to return to the menu. Then switch to the **STATISTICAL ANALYSIS** menu.

You should always check a collapsed variable against the original variable to make sure that you didn't make a mistake. *Select* **B. Tabular Statistics** and use **133** or **AGE!** as the row variable and **154** or **AGE COL** as the column variable. Do not select a control variable or a subset. Now scroll down the table and make sure that categories 18 through 29 of 133) AGE! are in category 1 of 154) AGE COL. Then check the accuracy for each of the remaining categories.

After you have completed these checks, the data will be ready to analyze.

NAME: _____

COURSE: _____

DATE: _____

EXERCISE

7

WORKSHEET

1. Based on what you learned from the textbook, discuss the problems with each of the following questions.

   a. *Question: During the past three years, have you done any of the following? (Circle all that apply.)*

      Voted in an election
      Tried to persuade someone about a political issue or candidate for public office
      Contributed money to a candidate for public office
      Written a letter to a public official about some political issue
      Worked in an election campaign

      What is the major problem with this question?

      How could this question be rewritten to eliminate the problem?

   b. *Question: Do you think that high schools should or should not be prohibited from banning the wearing of gang colors by students? (Circle one.)*   *Should   Should not*

      What is the major problem with this question?

      How could this question be rewritten to eliminate the problem?

c. *Question: Should judges be allowed to continue coddling criminals by giving some of them suspended sentences for the first offense? (Circle one.)*   *Yes   No*

What is the major problem with this question?

How could this question be rewritten to eliminate the problem?

d. *Question: What is your view concerning abortion? (Circle one.)*

   A. It should not be allowed.
   B. It should be allowed.

What is the major problem with this question?

How could this question be rewritten to eliminate the problem?

e. *Question: How many times have you changed your major since you began college? (Circle one.)*

                              0–2 times   3–5 times   More than 5 times

What is the major problem with this question?

How could this question be rewritten to eliminate the problem?

2. The following set of questions contains some contingency questions. In the column labeled Instructions, write appropriate instructions to an interviewer.

<u>Instructions</u>

```
1. Last week were you working full-time,
   part-time going to school, keeping
   house, or what?

   a. Working full-time

   b. Working part-time

   c. With a job but not at
      work because of temporary
      illness, vacation, strike

   d. Retired

   e. In school

   f. Keeping house

   g. OTHER

2. IF WORKING, FULL- OR PART-TIME:
   How many hours did you work last
   week, at all jobs?

3. IF WITH A JOB, BUT NOT AT WORK:
   How many hours a week do you
   usually work, at all jobs?

4. IF RETIRED, IN SCHOOL, KEEPING HOUSE,
   OR OTHER: Did you ever work for as
   long as one year?

   a. Yes    b. No
```

```
5. What kind of work (do you/did you)
   normally do? That is, what (is/was)
   your job called?

6. Were you born in this country?

   a. Yes    b. No
```

3. *Open* the data set **SURVEY**. (If your **SURVEY** data set is still open from the earlier portion of this exercise, you will need to remove the categories you temporarily assigned to missing data with the **F5** key. To remove them, *press* **F5**. *Type* **Y** and *press* *<ENTER>*. Delete all category names from this list and then *press* *<ENTER>* as many times as necessary to return to the menu.)

    a. What is the variable description of **31) EVER STRAY**?

       _____

       _____

    b. Select the **Univariate Statistics** task to look at the distribution of **31) EVER STRAY**.

CATEGORY LABEL	PERCENTAGE
1. _____	_____
2. _____	_____
3. _____	_____
5. _____	_____

    c. Which category should be treated as missing data in any analysis?

       _____

    d. Why are those who have never married placed in a separate category?

e. *Select* the **Tabular Statistics** task. Use **31** or **EVER STRAY** as the row variable and **7** or **OVER 50** as the column variable. Do not select a control variable. Use **31** or **EVER STRAY** as the subset variable—use **1** as the lower limit and **3** as the upper limit. Use column percentages and fill in the following table:

	UNDER 50	50 & OVER
YES		
NO		
NEVER WED		

$$V = \text{_____}$$

$$\text{Prob.} = \text{_____}$$

f. Use **31** or **EVER STRAY** as the row variable and **7** or **OVER 50** as the column variable. Do not select a control variable. Use **31** or **EVER STRAY** as the subset variable—use **1** as the lower limit and **2** as the upper limit. Use column percentages and fill in the following table:

	UNDER 50	50 & OVER
YES		
NO		

$$V = \text{_____}$$

$$\text{Prob.} = \text{_____}$$

g. Explain which table would be more appropriate for testing the hypothesis that individuals 50 and over are more likely to have strayed than are individuals under 50.

h. How was the strength of the relationship affected by which categories were treated as missing data?

4. a. Use the **Univariate Statistics** task to fill in the distribution of **152) PUB.DECIDE:**

         CATEGORY LABEL   PERCENTAGE

1. _____   _____

2. _____   _____

8. _____   _____

9. _____   _____

b. Which category should be treated as missing data in any analysis?

_____

c. The category "CAN'T CHOOSE" could be treated either as missing data or as a middle category between categories 1 and 2. (The collapse task may be used to drop categories and reorder categories, as well as combine categories.) Which option would you choose and why?

5. Sometimes the elimination of missing data can have a sizable impact on the results, either increasing the strength of the relationship or decreasing the strength.

a. *Select* the **Tabular Statistics** task. Use **152** or **PUB.DECIDE** as the row variable and **153** or **BUS.DECIDE** as the column variable. Use column percentaging to fill in the following table:

	BUSINESS D	GOV. LAWS	CAN'T CHOS	NO ANSWER
PEOPLE DEC				
GOV.LAWS				
CAN'T CHOS				
NO ANSWER				

$V = $ _____

Prob. = _____

b. Repeat this analysis, but select a subset. Use **152** or **PUB.DECIDE** as the first subset variable, and select **1** as the lower limit and **2** as the upper limit. Use **153** or **BUS.DECIDE** as the second subset variable, and select **1** as the lower limit and **2** as the upper limit. Use column percentaging to fill in the following table:

	BUSINESS D	GOV. LAWS
PEOPLE DEC		
GOV.LAWS		

$V = $ _____

Prob. = _____

c. How has the removal of these "missing data" categories affected the relationship?

6. The following paragraph describes a study conducted in 1935:

    *Long and Share Our Wealth stimulated the first scientific public opin-
    ion poll on a Presidential race. . . . Emil Hurja, the chief statistician and
    an executive director of the Democratic National Committee, mailed
    straw ballots and a cover letter on April 30, 1935 to about 150,000
    people in the U.S. states. He made the poll appear as if it were being con-
    ducted by a magazine, the nonexistent National Inquirer. All the informa-
    tion was to be received from a three-by-five inch card—the two-cents
    postage was prepaid.*[1]

    What element of this study might raise ethical questions? Explain.

---

[1] Edwin Amenta, Kathleen Dunleavy, and Mary Bernstein, "Huey Long's 'Share Our Wealth' and the
Second New Deal" American Sociological Review, Oct. 1994.

8

Comparative Methods

OVERVIEW

In this exercise, you will first learn more about selecting the proper base for the calculation of rates (e.g., average yearly food stamp benefit per recipient) in comparative research. Because comparative research often uses a relatively small number of cases, each individual case might have a substantial effect on the results. Thus, you will see the effect that outliers can have on correlations and how this problem can be handled. Lastly, you will see that missing data can be a major problem in comparative research.

BEFORE YOU BEGIN

Please make sure you have read Chapter 8 in the textbook and can answer the following review questions (you need not write any answers):

1. In comparative research, describe what a rate is and give examples of rates that have different kinds of bases.

2. Compare the reliability of aggregate data with that of survey data and explain why there is a difference.

3. What are the chief limitations of aggregate data based on official records?

4. If a rate such as a crime rate is not accurate, how can it still be useful for comparative research?

5. What is the difference between a case-oriented approach and variable-oriented research?

6. What are outliers and why is it important to check for their existence in comparative research results?

7. Why shouldn't you use 20 independent variables in a regression analysis to explain variation in welfare spending among the United States?

8. What are the primary kinds of circumstances in which ethical issues need to be considered in comparative research?

In this exercise, we'll explore some of the special problems of comparative research. First, choosing an appropriate base (or denominator) for a rate can be difficult, and different bases may lead to quite different results. Second, there are usually a limited number of cases in the data file, so the impact of each case is considerably greater than in survey research. Finally, there may be a sizable amount of missing data.

In comparative research, almost all the variables are rates of one type or another. In selecting the base (or denominator), you always should consider the concept you are trying to measure. In some situations, changing the base helps improve the validity of the measure. For example, dividing the number of students by the *school-age* population would be a better measure of current participation in the educational system than would dividing the number of students by the *total* population. If we used the total population to create this rate, then a country with a small number of school-age children would have a low rate, even if every child was enrolled in school. The difference between the crude birth rate and the fertility rate described in the textbook is another example of refining a rate by changing the base.

Sometimes, however, changing the base may completely change the concept being measured. For example, if you divide the number of female students by the number of females in the school-age population, you will obtain the proportion of *school-age females* who are enrolled in school. On the other hand, if you divide the number of female students by the total number of students, you will get the proportion of *students* who are female. Clearly, these are not the same, and countries would not necessarily rank in the same order on the two variables. Countries in which only the elite enrolled in school but that had no sex discrimination would have a relatively low proportion of school-age females enrolled in school, but a relatively high proportion of students would be female.

Rates may change (or differ) because the values of either the denominator or the numerator or both change. Consider, for example, the percentage of deaths between ages 15 and 25 attributable to suicide. The numerator is the number of deaths by suicide in this age group, and the denominator is the total number of deaths in this age group. The rate can increase because the number of suicides increases, or because the number of deaths from other causes decreases, or both. If we are interested in the propensity of this age group to commit suicide, a better base would be the number of persons between the ages of 15 and 25.

Note: Very small numbers and very large numbers are difficult to read. Consequently, most rates are adjusted so that the values fall in the range from 0 to 100. For example, rather than calculate the proportion of the population that was murdered (which would give extremely small numbers), we use the number of murders per 100,000 population. This is just the proportion murdered multiplied by 100,000. On the other hand, reporting the number of males per 100,000 population would create undesirably large numbers, so the percentage male—the proportion multiplied by 100—is usually used. Multiplying (or dividing) a rate by a constant value has no effect on the results.

Let's look at how using different bases in constructing rates can affect the results. Start MicroCase and open the **USA** data set. The variable 125) FS$/PER uses the amount spent on the food stamp program as the numerator and the number of recipients of food stamps as the denominator for each state—so it is the average benefit per recipient. The variable 126) FS$/CAP uses the same numerator but uses the population of the state as the base, or denominator—so it is the average benefit cost per capita. Let's see if this difference in bases has any effect on relationships with other variables.

Select the **Scatterplot** task. Use **126** or **FS$/CAP** as the dependent variable and **86** or **% POOR** as the independent variable. This scatterplot is shown in Figure 8.1—the correlation is .807 and significant.

Figure 8.1   Scatterplot between 126) FS$/CAP and 86) % POOR

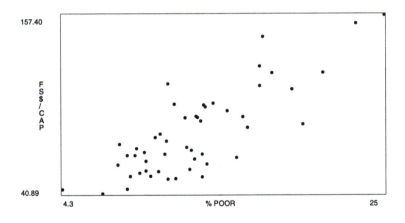

Now create a scatterplot between **125** or **FS$/PER** and **86** or **% POOR**—the plot is shown in Figure 8.2. The correlation is .044 and not significant. Notice the case at the top of the screen. Removing this case from the scatterplot might have a sizable impact on the scatterplot.

We can use the outlier task to see if there is any single case that is making a substantial difference in the correlation coefficient. *Press* **O** to see the effect of this outlier. The case at the top now flashes. This case has been identified as the case that would have the greatest effect on the correlation coefficient if it were removed. We can see below the scatterplot that this case is Hawaii and that removal of this case would change the correlation coefficient from 0.044 to 0.120.

The correlation would still not be significant. So there would be no reason to remove the outlier. *Press <ENTER> to return to the task.*

Clearly in this example, one would reach quite different conclusions by using the cost per participant than by using the cost per capita. Poorer states spend more on food stamps per capita, probably reflecting that a greater percentage of the population receives food stamps. However, the poverty of the state does not appear to affect the amount received by the average recipient. We might speculate that the cost per recipient is a function of the food costs of the states. States in which food is more expensive will give greater benefits per recipient than will states in which food is less expensive. Let's see if we can check this idea.

Figure 8.2   Scatterplot between 125)FS$/PER and 86) % POOR

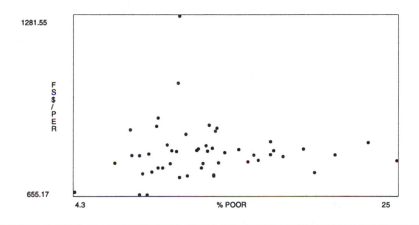

We don't have a measure of the cost of food readily available, but we do have information on median rents. Generally, both rent and food reflect the relative cost of living. Let's look at the relationship between 125) FS$/PER and 83) RENT. In the scatterplot task, use **125** or **FS$/PER** as the dependent variable and **83** or **RENT** as the independent variable. The resulting plot is shown in Figure 8.3.

Figure 8.3   Scatterplot between 125) FS$/PER and 83) RENT

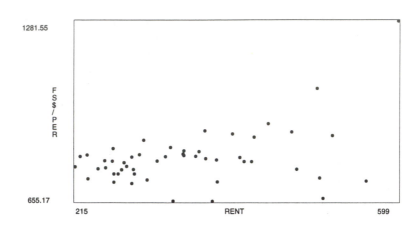

The correlation is .418 and significant. However, there is a case in the upper right corner—would removing this case have a significant impact on the correlation coefficient?

Press **O** to see the effect of the outlier. The outlier is Hawaii, and removal of this case would change the correlation from .418 to .235 and change the significance level from .001 to .105—from significant at the .01 level to not significant. *Press* **Y** to remove Hawaii. Alaska is now the outlier. Removal of Alaska would change the correlation to .122 and the significance level to .407. When Hawaii and Alaska are removed, there is no correlation between the two variables. This suggests that either food costs do not affect the size of food stamp benefits or median rent is not a good substitute for the cost of food.

The impact of Hawaii on this correlation coefficient demonstrates another frequent problem in comparative research. Because of the relatively small number of cases, a single case may have a sizable impact on the results. The wise comparative researcher will learn something about the units being used before beginning the actual analysis. In our example, if we knew that food costs for the 48 contiguous states had little variation, and food in Alaska and Hawaii was much more expensive, we would be better able to interpret the results. Similarly, if you are using a data set of nations, you should be aware that Singapore and Hong Kong are frequently included as cases in such data sets. However, these are "city-nations"—the boundaries of the city and the boundaries of the nation are the same. Since these cases have virtually no rural or farm areas, they are going to differ in many ways from other nations. Such deviant cases can have sizable effects on the results of an analysis.

With MicroCase, you can determine that an outlier is having a significant impact, but such a determination will not explain why the case is so deviant. In our example, we don't know why Hawaii is so different from the other cases and, consequently, we have no justification for removing Hawaii from the analysis.

If you have no idea why a particular case would be an outlier, you should double-check the data for that case. First, check the data values for the case against the original source. Perhaps the data were not entered correctly. Even if the data match the source, perhaps the source is incorrect—data are often misprinted or reported incorrectly. Try to find a second source for the data. If the two sources have decidedly different values, you must then determine which is the better source.

In some situations, you will know exactly why a case is an outlier. The results with that case removed may better reflect the overall relationship. You are then justified in removing that case from the analysis. Be sure to report any cases removed from analysis. In some situations, you may want to report the results both with and without the suspect case.

Removing a case from the analysis essentially assigns the missing data value to all variables for that case. This leads us to a third major difficulty in comparative research. Even without removing cases, comparative data sets frequently have a great deal of missing data—even worse, the cases with missing data almost never represent a random selection. For example, prior to the collapse of the Soviet bloc, data were much more difficult to find for Eastern European countries than for the other European countries. Similarly, data for less developed countries are more likely to be incomplete than are data for more developed countries. In the written exercises, you'll get a chance to see how missing data can influence the results.

Your turn.

1. You want to determine the college graduation rate by state. Which would be the better base, the total population of the state or the population over age 25? (Circle one.)

Total population   Population over age 25

Explain your answer.

2. You are interested in voter turnout by state in the last presidential election. Obviously, the numerator for the rate would be the number of persons in each state who voted in that election. List three possible bases, or denominators, that could be used for creating a rate.

a. _____

b. _____

c. _____

Circle the letter of the rate you think would be best and explain why you think it would be the best.

3. *Open* the **USA** data set. *Press* **F3** to open the codebook window.

    a. What is the description for **63) %FEMALE LG**?

    _____

    _____

    b. According to the description, what numerator was used in calculating this rate?

    _____

    c. According to the description, what base, or denominator, was used in calculating this rate?

    _____

    d. Why wasn't the population of the state used as the base?

4. Traffic statistics use different bases. For example, traffic fatalities can be reported as number of fatalities per 1,000 population, number of fatalities per 1,000 licensed drivers, number of fatalities per 1,000 registered vehicles, and so on. In the **USA** data set, you have two measures of the amount of driving in each state: **127) MILES/DRV.** and **128) MILES/VHCL.**

    a. Look at the description of each of these variables and describe the difference in how they are calculated.

b. *Select* the **Scatterplot** task. *Select* **70** or **PICKUPS** as the dependent variable and **127** or **MILES/DRV.** as the independent variable.

r = _____

Prob. = _____

Press **O** to identify the case that has the greatest impact on the correlation coefficient. If this case were removed, what would the results be?

r = _____

Prob. = _____

Should you consider removing the outlier? (Circle one.)   Yes   No

c. *Select* **70** or **PICKUPS** as the dependent variable and **128** or **MILES/VHCL.** as the independent variable.

r = _____

Prob. = _____

Press **O** to identify the case that has the greatest impact on the correlation coefficient. If this case were removed, what would the results be?

r = _____

Prob. = _____

Should you consider removing the outlier? (Circle one.)   Yes   No

d. Why does the relationship with **70) PICKUPS** differ depending on which measure is used? (Comparing the maps of these variables might help you answer this question.)

e. *Select* the **Scatterplot** task. *Select* **127** or **MILES/DRV.** as the dependent variable and **129** or **CARS/HSE90** as the independent variable.

What is the description of **129) CARS/HSE90**? (*Press* **X** to see the description.)

_____

_____

r = _____

Prob. = _____

Use the outlier option to identify the case that has the greatest impact on the correlation coefficient. If this case were removed, what would the results be?

r = _____

Prob. = _____

Should you consider removing the outlier? (Circle one.)   Yes   No

f. *Select* **128** or **MILES/VHCL.** as the dependent variable and **129** or **CARS/HSE90** as the independent variable.

r = _____

Prob. = _____

Press **O** to identify the case that has the greatest impact on the correlation coefficient. If this case were removed, what would the results be?

r = _____

Prob. = _____

Should you consider removing the outlier? (Circle one.)   Yes   No

g. Why does the relationship with **129) CARS/HSE90** differ depending on which rate is used? (Comparing the maps of these variables might help you answer this question.)

5. Sometimes, researchers will include Washington, D.C., in a data set with the 50 states. *Open* the data set named **US&DC**.

   a. *Select* the **Scatterplot** task. Use **3** or **%GRAD.DEG** as the dependent variable and **2** or **%BLACK90** as the independent variable.

   r = _____

   Prob. = _____

   b. *Press* **O** to identify the case that has the greatest impact on the correlation coefficient.

   Name of outlier: _____

   r = _____

   Prob. = _____

   c. Should you consider removing the outlier? (Circle one.)   Yes   No

   d. What is your conclusion about the relationship between these two variables?

6. With the **US&DC** data set, use **4** or **ONE P.HH90** as the dependent variable and **3** or **%GRAD.DEG** as the independent variable.

   a. What is the description of **4) ONE P.HH90**? (*Press* **Y** to see the description.)

   _____

   _____

   r = _____

   Prob. = _____

b. *Press* **O** to identify the case that has the greatest impact on the correlation coefficient.

Name of outlier: _____

r = _____

Prob. = _____

c. Should you consider removing the outlier? (Circle one.)   Yes   No

d. What is your conclusion about the relationship between these two variables?

e. Would you advise researchers to include Washington, D.C., in a data set on the states of the United States? (Circle one.)   Yes   No

Explain your answer below.

7. The correlation function in the student version of MicroCase has been set to use listwise deletion of missing data. This means that, if a case has missing data on *any* of the variables included in the analysis, that case will be excluded from *all* correlations. *Open* the **USA** data set. Note that the missing data value is –99. *Select* the **Mapping** Function and map **51** or **% FAT**. *Press* **D** (for Distribution).

a. Which case(s) has (have) missing data on this variable?

b. Map **80** or **FOODSTAMPS**. Which case(s) has (have) missing data on this variable?

c. Map **92** or **MATH SCORE**. Which case(s) has (have) missing data on this variable?

d. *Select* the **Correlation** task. Correlate variables **51) % FAT** and **80) FOOD-STAMPS**.

What is the correlation between these two variables? _____

How many cases are used in the calculation?_____

Which cases are excluded?

e. Now correlate variables **80) FOODSTAMPS** and **92) MATH SCORE**.

What is the correlation between these two variables? _____

How many cases are used in the calculation?_____

Which cases are excluded?

f. Now examine the correlations among all three variables at once and fill in the following correlation matrix:

	80) FOODSTAMPS	92) MATH SCORE	51) % FAT
80) FOODSTAMPS			
92) MATH SCORE			
51) % FAT			

How many cases are used in these calculations? _____

g. Do the results change when all three variables are in the matrix (compared with the results using only two variables)? If so, how?

h. Explain why researchers should be careful when working with data sets that contain considerable missing data.

Field Methods

OVERVIEW

In this exercise, you will learn more about problems and issues in field research. Field research is less structured than other methods, and this has both advantages and disadvantages. You will see that field researchers must be careful not to let this lack of structure undermine their studies.

BEFORE YOU BEGIN

Please make sure you have read Chapter 9 in the textbook and can answer the following review questions (you need not write any answers):

1. When is field research better than other methods of social research?

2. Why is reliability often low in field studies and how can it be increased?

3. Discuss the two major problems involved in entering the field.

4. What is the difference between structured and unstructured observation?

5. What are informants in field research? What are the advantages and disadvantages of using informants?

6. Describe field notes and the general processes by which they are analyzed.

7. What are the primary ethical concerns in field research?

Field research is considerably less structured than other types of social research. In survey research, we can look at how the sample was selected and at the questions asked. In comparative research, we can determine whether a particular rate appears to be an acceptable measure. But, in reports of field research, we have virtually no means of checking on the accuracy of the observations. This is why most field studies are exploratory, rather than hypothesis testing. In this exercise, we'll see some special problems that are created by this lack of structure.

One of the first problems is that different observers focus on different elements. For example, consider something as uncomplicated as a group of people talking with one another. One researcher might focus on the content of the conversation, while another might be more interested in nonverbal communication. Differences of style between males and females might be the main interest of another. Decoding the influence, or power structure, of the group might be another focus. Obviously, the interest of the researcher will influence what is observed and recorded, as well as what is not observed and not recorded. Of course, the purpose of field research is not only to observe, but also to organize and interpret these observations in a meaningful way.

Unfortunately, many researchers not only have certain interests, but also have developed definite opinions on a topic. For example, the researcher interested in gender styles of interaction already may believe that females will be submissive and males will be dominant. Bias—either intentional or unintentional—is almost certain to creep into this study. This researcher already has a hypothesis and is not using field research to explore gender styles in interaction but rather to document preconceived differences. This is not exploratory research but hypothesis-testing research. In this situation, other methods better suited to hypothesis testing would be more appropriate—content analysis of videotaped conversations might be one such approach.

At the other extreme, researchers who observe without any preconceived structure whatsoever are bound to be buried in a sea of unrelated details and accomplish nothing. Thus the problem for the field researcher is to focus the study without predetermining its outcome.

Characteristics of the researcher also can have a major effect on the subjects of observation. An individual's actions are frequently influenced by who is watching. All of us engage in private behaviors that we would not want observed. We behave differently in front of our boss than we do in front of a subordinate. Age, gender, attractiveness, and many other characteristics of the observer can influence the behavior of those being observed. A 20-year-old woman and a 50-year-old man observing the same group might reach quite different conclusions since the behavior of the group may be affected by who is watching. In Japan, even the spoken language differs greatly according to the gender of the speaker. That is, men and women have different accents. This led to considerable embarrassment for some World War II American GIs who learned the language from their Japanese girlfriends. This is another reason that having more than one observer is a good idea.

Obviously, the effects of observer characteristics will be even more pronounced when informers are involved. In some societies, age, gender, and marital status determine interaction patterns—some members may not even be permitted to talk with the observer.

Field research also may be applied research. A researcher might observe the operation of a ward in a hospital. Sometimes, such studies are unstructured. For example, the researcher may discover that doctor/nurse conflicts are having a negative impact on patient care. More often, they are studies to *evaluate* an organization or process. The researchers already have a model about what "should" happen. The observations are used to determine the extent to which this "model" is being met. For example, business consultants frequently observe the operation of a company for a period of time in order to recommend changes that might improve the operation of the business. Typically, such researchers already know how "good" companies work—for example, that employees are sharing in the decision-making. Their observations are used to determine how the company should be changed to match this preconceived ideal. Such studies may be very useful for the organizations involved, but they are not social science.

NAME: _____

COURSE: _____

DATE: _____

Workbook exercises and software are copyrighted. Copying is prohibited by law.

EXERCISE

9

WORKSHEET

1. Look at this photograph of new recruits to the Marine Corps to answer these questions:

   a. How would a field researcher obtain access to this setting?

b. Boot camp is eight weeks long. What problems does this pose for the researcher?

c. What characteristics of the researcher might affect his or her success in completing a study in this setting?

d. Discuss the relative value of a new recruit versus that of an instructor as an informer.

e. List four different topics that a field researcher might study in Marine basic training.

   1.

   2.

   3.

   4.

f. What problems exist for taking field notes in a study of basic training?

g. If the recruits were female, how would this affect the research project?

2.   An anthropologist made the following statement:

> "I know that the women are behaving normally around me because when my husband and I are talking with them, their behavior changes when he leaves."

Do you agree with her conclusion? Why or why not?

3.   a. A team of researchers are interested in studying the role of house-husband/stay-at-home dad. They are especially interested in how this role differs from that of the housewife/stay-at-home mother. How would you design a field study to explore this topic?

   b. List three problems the field researchers are likely to encounter and how you would solve them.

      1.

      2.

3.

4. Consider the following potential "informers" in the studies given. Discuss the pluses and minuses of trusting the information of each informer listed.

   a. **In a study of interpersonal relationships in an inner-city neighborhood:**

   An elderly woman who spends most of her time watching the street from her window

   A teenage boy who goes to high school, plays on a neighborhood baseball team, and watches TV in the evenings

   A full-time, employed adult who frequently has dealt with city bureaucrats regarding neighborhood issues and problems

   A mother who spends each day in the neighborhood park with her two infants

   b. **In a study of a school for rebellious teenagers:**

   The father of a recent graduate who appears to have become better adjusted

A student who was dismissed for incorrigible behavior

A long-time instructor at the school

The director of a similar, competing school

The full-time maintenance man who lives on the school campus

The counselor who meets with each student once a week to assess progress

5. A researcher pretends to be a supporter in order to infiltrate an antigovernment organization that sometimes commits illegal acts. What ethical problems are most relevant here?

6. A social scientist who is a member of an organization decides to do a field study of this organization and receives funding from the organization for the study. Describe the problems in this situation.

Experimental Methods

OVERVIEW

In this exercise, you will learn more about the necessary conditions for an experiment and about the power of the experiment in eliminating sources of spuriousness in relationships. You also will gain experience in designing experimental research and drawing the proper conclusions from the results.

BEFORE YOU BEGIN

Please make sure you have read Chapter 10 in the textbook and can answer the following review questions (you need not write any answers):

1. What are the two essential characteristics of true experiments?

2. Compare the advantages and disadvantages of laboratory experiments and field experiments.

3. What is the difference between an experimental group and a control group?

4. What is a double-blind experiment and what use does it serve?

5. How can experiments be used in surveys?

6. What two primary sources of bias in experiments can reduce reliability?

7. Why is it important to make sure in an experiment that the independent variable really varied in the way it was supposed to vary?

8. Describe how each of the following factors can affect the results of quasi-experiments: history, maturation, testing effects, instrument effects, regression to the mean, and selection bias.

9. What is subject "mortality" and how can it affect experimental results?

10. What are the primary ethical concerns in experimental research?

The social scientists who designed the questionnaire for the 1994 General Social Survey were interested in how question wordings on government spending might affect the responses—would relatively minor changes in the phrasing of questions have a significant impact on the distribution of responses? They recognized that an experiment would be the best method for testing for such an effect. Half of the survey respondents, randomly selected, would be given one question wording, and the other half would be given the second question wording. The responses of the two groups could then be compared. So the independent variable would be the question wording—there are two different treatment conditions represented by the two different wordings. The dependent variable would be the response to the question. By comparing the responses of subjects in the two treatment conditions, researchers could tell whether question wording had an effect.

Let's take a look at the results of this experiment. Because the GSS is a survey, the GSS data file is organized in a manner appropriate for survey analysis. Consequently, we have created a data set better organized for experimental analysis.

Start MicroCase and *open* **EXPER**. *Press* **F3** to look at the variable list. The value of the first variable is the experimental condition for that subject—were they asked the first wording of the question or the second wording? The second variable is the response to the first question. The first treatment used the following wording: Are we spending too much, too little, or about the right amount on *welfare*? The second treatment had different wording: Are we spending too much, too little, or about the right amount on *assistance to the poor*? We want to compare the responses of those in treatment 1 with the responses of those in treatment 2. You can see that there are a series of additional questions about spending in which the wording differed slightly between the two treatment conditions. So, in fact, we have a series of experiments.

Because the cases were *randomly assigned* to conditions, other characteristics of the cases will not be correlated with the independent variable (i.e., the question wording). We can see this by looking at the cross-tabulation of the treatment variable with these other characteristics. *Select* the **Tabular Statistics** task. Use **13** or **SEX** as the row variable and **1** or **TREATMENT** as the column variable. Do not select a control variable or a subset variable. Use column percentaging.

	Row Variable: 13) SEX	Column Variable: 1) TREATMENT
	ONE	TWO
MALE	43.9	42.3
FEMALE	56.1	57.7

We can see that the distribution of sex is almost identical in the two conditions—43.9 percent of the subjects in the first condition and 42.3 percent of the subjects in the second condition were male. Other characteristics of the subjects would also be about the same across the two conditions. The fact that the independent variable is uncorrelated with other characteristics of the subjects is the strength of experimental research. Remember that, for a third variable to make a relationship spurious, that variable must be correlated with both the independent and dependent variables. So in experiments we do not have to worry about possible sources of spuriousness. We only need to examine the relationship between the independent and dependent variables to support or reject our research hypothesis.

Now use **2** or **WELFARE** as the row variable and **1** or **TREATMENT** as the column variable. Use column percentages. We can see that 13.3 percent of those shown the first wording thought too little was being spent, while 59.3 percent of those in the second treatment condition felt this way. *Press* **S** to look at the statistics. We can see that the results are statistically significant. So the difference in wording did have an effect on the subject's view toward government spending.

If we can assume that the dependent variable is measured at the interval or ratio level, there is another technique that can be used in experimental analysis. Analysis of variance is similar to regression analysis except the independent variable is nominal, or categorical. To demonstrate this technique, we'll assume that the dependent variables are close enough to interval to justify its use.

Return to the **STATISTICAL ANALYSIS** menu and *select* **C. Analysis of Variance**. Use **2** or **WELFARE** as the dependent variable and **1** or **TREATMENT** as the independent variable. Do not select a subset. In a few moments a graphic similar to the one in Figure 10.1 will appear.

Figure 10.1   Box-and-Whisker Diagram of 2) WELFARE by 1) TREATMENT

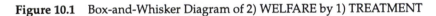

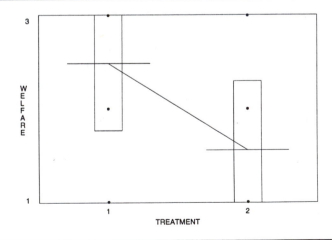

This is called a box-and-whisker diagram. It is just a scatterplot between the two variables with some additional information. The independent variable, treatment condition, is shown across the bottom. Those in the first treatment condition are shown at the left, and those in the second treatment condition are shown at the right. The vertical axis represents the dependent variable. In this example, there are only three possible values for this variable, so there are many cases at each of the three levels but only one dot. So far, this is just the same as a scatterplot.

Since the independent variable in analysis of variance is categorical, we can provide additional information about the dependent variable within each of these categories. We can calculate the mean and variation of the dependent variable within each category of the independent variable. The vertical box shown at the left represents the variation in the dependent variable for the first condition. The horizontal line (the whisker) in the middle of this box represents the mean of the dependent variable. The box at the right shows the same information for the second condition. A line connects the means of the two conditions. In this example, there is a sizable difference in the means.

Press **A** to see the analysis of variance table. This is similar to the analysis of variance table shown for regression. For our needs, we can ignore all the information except the significance level (Prob. = 0.000) and the value of eta-squared, 0.289. Eta-squared is a measure of association and tells us the strength of the relationship between the two variables.[1] In this example, this relationship is highly significant.

Press **M** to see the mean of the dependent variable for each condition. For the 1,457 cases in the first treatment condition, the mean was 2.486—in the middle between the categories "right" and "too much." For the 1,394 cases in the second condition, the mean was 1.557—in between the categories "too little" and "right."

Return to the beginning of the task and *select* **3** or **SPACE PRG** as the dependent variable and **1** or **TREATMENT** as the independent variable. In this example, the line that connects the means is horizontal. There is virtually no difference between the conditions. If you look at the analysis of variance table, you see that the results are not significant (shown as *Prob.* = *n.s.*) and eta-squared is zero. Return to the beginning of the task.

Now *select* **4** or **HEALTH** as the dependent variable and **1** or **TREATMENT** as the independent variable. The line connecting means is almost horizontal. *Press* **M** to look at the actual means. Treatment 1 with 1,448 cases has a mean of 1.419, while treatment 2 with 1,380 cases has a mean of 1.483. Not much difference. Now

---

[1] Eta and r, the Pearson correlation coefficient, are based on the same mathematical ideas except that r assumes that the relationship will be linear and eta has no restrictions on the nature of the relationship.

press **A** to look at the analysis of variance table. Eta-squared is .002 and is significant at the .05 level. How can such a weak relationship be significant?

Remember that statistical significance tells us only that it is likely a relationship exists in the population. Two elements affect this level: the strength of the relationship in the sample and the size of the sample. In this study, the sample size is extremely large so that even a small relationship is likely to be significant. Again this demonstrates why we should look at both the significance level and the strength of the relationship. The eta-squared of .002 tells us that, while a relationship may exist in the population, it is a very weak relationship.

We can see that the analysis of experiments is much simpler than the analysis of surveys because we need not worry about sources of spuriousness.

What do these results tell us? Simply that relatively minor changes in wording can have a significant effect on responses. (We examined this issue in a slightly different way in Exercise 3.) Suppose that instead of doing an experiment, researchers had used one set of question wordings in the GSS one year and the other set of wordings the next year. If we observed a difference in the responses between the two years, we could not be sure that it was caused by the change in question wordings. It is possible that the attitudes in the population actually changed during the year. By using an experiment, we have eliminated any such alternative explanations and can be sure that the question wordings themselves are causing the differences.

This experiment is unusual in that a probability sample of a particular population provided the subjects for the experiment. This means that the results of this study can be generalized to the relevant population. However, this isn't really very important because our interest wasn't in this specific population but in the more general issue of the importance of question wordings. The use of a probability sample also means that it is possible to examine the effect of other variables, such as education, income, and race, on attitudes toward spending. Such analysis, of course, would be regular survey analysis and you would have to consider possible sources of spuriousness.

Your turn.

NAME: _____

COURSE: _____

DATE: _____

EXERCISE

10

WORKSHEET

1. Two social scientists were interested in studying the effect of sex education on sexual behavior. They selected a school in which some of the students would be participating in a sex education study during the year while others would be taking a computer literacy course. (Parents selected one or the other of these courses for their children.) The researchers administered a questionnaire on sexual behavior at the end of the year and found that students who had taken the sex education sequence were much more likely to be sexually active than were the other students. They concluded that sex education increases the sexual activity of preteens.

   a. Given the design of this study, can we have any confidence in the conclusion? (Circle one.)   Yes   No

   When the researchers were told that this was not an experiment, they responded, "That's OK. It's a quasi-experiment."

   b. Describe why this study is not a true experiment.

   c. Provide another explanation for why the researchers found the two groups to differ in sexual activity.

d. Assume that the researchers' hypothesis was that taking a sex education class would increase the sexual activity of the participants. How could they have designed a true experiment to test this hypothesis?

e. What ethical problems would the researchers encounter in this study and how could they solve them?

2. The text describes an experiment in which students are randomly assigned to an experimental group that, over a period of six months, watches a series of movies designed to reduce racial prejudice or to a control group that does not watch the movies.

a. Suppose a large number of subjects dropped out of the experimental condition—they stopped staying after school to watch the movies. What problem would this introduce in reaching a conclusion about the effect of the movies?

b. How could the design of the experiment be changed to minimize this problem?

c. Suppose that on the posttest there was no difference in racial prejudice between the two groups—individuals in both groups were extremely low in prejudice. In addition, there was no change between pretest and posttest for individuals in either group. Would this indicate that the movies had no effect on prejudice? Why or why not?

d. How could this study be modified to provide a better test of the effectiveness of the movies?

e. Suppose that on the posttest there was no difference in racial prejudice between the two groups—individuals in both groups were low in prejudice. However, in both groups, there was a big decrease in racial prejudice between the pretest and the posttest for each individual. Analyzing the friendship structure and interpersonal contact among all subjects, the researchers find that subjects in the control group had many friends and a great deal of interpersonal contact with subjects in the experimental group. How might this fact have affected the results of the study?

f. How could this study be modified to eliminate this problem?

3. *Open* the data file **EXPER**. *Select* the **Tabular Statistics** task. Use **14** or **RACE** as the dependent variable and **1** or **TREATMENT** as the independent variable. Use column percentaging to fill in the following table:

	ONE	TWO
WHITE		
BLACK		
OTHER		

V = _____

Prob. = _____

Why is the racial distribution so similar across the two treatment conditions?

4. Now *select* the **Analysis of Variance** task. Variables 5 to 12 were also part of the methodological experiment.

   a. *Select* one variable from this set as the dependent variable and use **1) TREATMENT** as the independent variable.

   Which variable did you select?   _____

   What is the description of this variable?

   _____

   _____

   What is the mean of each group?:

   Treatment 1: mean is _____

   Treatment 2: mean is _____

   Is this difference statistically significant? (Circle one.)   Yes   No

   b. *Select* a second variable from this set and conduct the exact same analysis.

   Which variable did you select?   _____

   What is the description of this variable?

   _____

   _____

   What is the mean of each group?:

   Treatment 1: mean is _____

   Treatment 2: mean is _____

   Is this difference statistically significant? (Circle one.)   Yes   No

5. Assuming that you had a large group of volunteers for an experiment, design an experiment to test whether reading newspaper editorials affects the opinions of people on social, political, and economic issues. Following the example described in Design 4 in the textbook, present a diagram along with your description of the research design.

6. In the first class session for a course, the professor announces that each person in the class has been randomly assigned to one of two groups, A or B. Group A will use the regular textbook for the course, but group B will use a computerized tutorial—a tutorial that the professor has developed and believes will greatly increase student learning while also making it much more enjoyable. The two groups will otherwise receive the same treatment (same lectures, exams, etc.). The professor announces that the purpose of this experiment is to determine whether the computerized tutorial increases learning. At the end of the course, the professor will compare the exam scores of the two groups to determine whether the computerized tutorial was better than the textbook.

    a. Describe how subject bias (demand characteristics) could be a problem here.

    b. Describe how experimenter bias could be a problem here.

    c. What ethical issue might be raised by some of the students in the course? How might this problem be resolved?

11

Content Analysis

OVERVIEW

In this exercise, you will learn more about content analysis by doing a small content analysis of newspaper personal ads in which people are trying to meet people of the opposite sex. You actually will code some of the variables and then test several hypotheses based on the data file.

BEFORE YOU BEGIN

Please make sure you have read Chapter 11 in the textbook and can answer the following review questions (you need not write any answers):

1. What is content analysis and what kinds of materials can be used in such analysis?

2. What is the difference between manifest content and latent content?

3. Describe the two primary factors that determine reliability in content analysis.

4. How do deposit bias and survival bias affect the validity of content analysis?

5. What does it mean to say that content analysis is a form of unobtrusive measurement?

The unit of analysis in content analysis is not an individual, nor even a collection of individuals, but rather a cultural artifact. However, the basic steps of the research process remain the same. After identifying the topic of interest and developing the research hypotheses, the researcher selects an appropriate sample of cases (artifacts), develops measures of the concepts (the coding system), collects the data (codes the cases), and tests the hypotheses.

In this exercise, you will apply content analysis to personal ads in which people are seeking to meet persons of the opposite sex. These ads were selected from one issue of a daily newspaper in the Pacific Northwest. In this particular newspaper, the newspaper ads are free. Each advertiser records a voice greeting that plays when an interested person calls the published number. Those who respond to the ads pay $1.99 per minute to hear the message at the 1-900 number and to leave a message for the advertiser.

Since there were an equal number of male and female ads, a stratified random sampling design was used. The ads were first divided into those placed by men and those placed by women. Then 50 ads were selected randomly from each gender group. The ads included in the sample are reprinted at the end of this discussion—the first 50 are males and the second 50 are females.

Most of the ads provide information about the ad writer and describe characteristics of the person they are seeking. The content of these ads can be coded easily. In fact, if you look at the top of page , you'll see that some elements already have been coded by the advertiser. For example, W means "white," C means "Christian," LTR means "long-term relationship," and so on. Looking over the ads, we decided upon the following variables and categories:

GENDER
Gender of advertiser:
>   1—male, 2—female

AGE-AD
Age of advertiser:
>   1—under 40, 2—40 & over, 3—not stated
>   If range given, code youngest end.

AGE-DES
Age desired:
>   1—under 40, 2—40 & over, 3—not stated
>   If range given, code youngest end.

LTR
Long-term relationship (LTR):
>   1—LTR stated, 2—not clear, 3—no long term
>   If indicate "friends first," code as 2.

SEXUAL IMP
Sexual implication:
>1—explicit, 2—implicit, 3—none
>If indicate "friends first," code as 3.

APPEAR-AD
Physical description of advertiser:
>1—none provided, 2—minimal description provided (e.g., height/weight proportionate or height), 3—stresses attractiveness (e.g., cute, beautiful, handsome, good looking)

APPEAR-DES
Physical description desired:
>1—none provided, 2—minimal description provided (e.g., height/weight proportionate or height), 3—stresses attractiveness (e.g., cute, beautiful, handsome, good looking)

SECUR
Financial security desired:
>1—stated, 2—none indicated
>If seeking professional, code as 1.

ACTIVE
Stresses active lifestyle:
>1—yes, 2—no

Start MicroCase and *open* the **CONTENT** data file. Each case is one of the ads. The order of the cases matches that of the list of ads. Use **F3** to open the codebook window. You can see that the variables already have been defined and, in fact, data have been entered for most of these variables. *Press <ENTER>* to close the codebook window.

Let's look at the coding of the first case:

1. CHRISTIAN AND KIND
SWM, 23, Christian values, 6'1", physically fit, attractive, enjoys summer activities, beaches, conversation. Would like to meet a Christian female for friendship, possibly more.

To look at the coding for the first case, *select* **D. List or Print Variable Values** from the **DATA AND FILE MANAGEMENT** menu. *Type* **1** and *press <ENTER>* to have the information sent to the screen. *Type* **1** and *press <ENTER>* to select the first case and *type* **1–9** and *press <ENTER>* to select the first nine variables. *Press <ENTER>* to see the data. (This task may be slow on your computer.)

We now can examine the codes for each variable. (Use the right arrow key to move to the variables not currently showing.) Gender has been coded 1 for male, age of advertiser has been coded as 1 for under 40, desired age is not stated so it is coded as 3. The ad states that the advertiser is looking for "friendship, possibly more." This is coded as a 2 according to the "friendship first" note for variable 4. There are no sexual implications in the ad so variable 5, SEXUAL IMP, is coded 3. The advertiser describes himself as "attractive"—this places him in category 3 of variable 6, APPEAR-AD. He mentions neither the appearance nor the financial security of the person he is seeking, so variable 7, APPEAR-DES, is coded as 1 and variable 8, SECUR, is coded as 2. Finally, he is coded as 1 on variable 9, ACTIVE. If you were to list the data for all cases, you would see that each case has already been coded for these first nine variables. *Press <ENTER>* to return to the main menu.

We're going to test the hypothesis that the sex of the advertiser affects the content of the ads. But first, we need to determine if our coding is reliable enough for analysis. In a previous exercise, you learned how to use rekey verification to increase the accuracy of data entry from questionnaires. Rekey verification is useful for checking data entry mistakes—the correct value is obvious. In content analysis, the "correct" answer is subject to interpretation. The researcher wants to be able to compare the data from multiple coders and assess the degree of concensus. Data from each of the coders must be available to the researcher, so rekey verification is not an appropriate technique. Instead, each additional coder should enter data into new variables.

If you press the **F3** key, you can see that there are nine additional variables in this data set. No data have been entered for these variables so they currently contain the missing data code for each case. In the exercises, you'll be asked to code several cases on some of these variables, so let's quickly see how to enter the data using MicroCase.

From the **DATA AND FILE MANAGEMENT** menu *select* **C. Enter Data from Keyboard**. *Type* **1** and *press <ENTER>* to enter data by row. *Press <ENTER>* to accept the prompt to enter new data. *Type* **1–2** and *press <ENTER>* to select the first two cases. *Type* **10–18** and *press <ENTER> twice* to enter data for variables 10 through 18. You now can enter data for the first two cases on these nine variables. We already have discussed the first case—go ahead and re-enter those codes at this point. For each variable, just type the appropriate code and press <ENTER>. (If you need to move backward to a previous variable entry, *press* the **SHIFT** and **TAB** keys together.) After you enter the last variable, you'll be moved to the second case.

Let's take a look at the second case:

2. CHRISTIAN IN SEATTLE
Attractive, Christian SWM, 28, 6', H/W proportionate, active person, financially secure, stable and healthy. Would like to meet Christian female, for friendship, possibly more.

This is very similar to the first ad. Referring back to our original coding scheme, we'll code 1 for GENDER1, 1 for AGE-AD1, and 3 for AGE-DES1. Again the phrase "friendship, possibly more" leads us to code 2 for LTR1 and 3 for SEXUAL IM1. The advertiser provides a minimal physical description (6', H/W proportionate) but does not stress attractiveness—code 2 for APPEAR-AD1. He neither provides a physical description of the person sought (code 1 for APPEAR-DE1) nor requests financial security (code 2 for SECUR1). He does indicate an active lifestyle—code 1 for ACTIVE. You now have completed coding for the first two cases. *Press <ENTER>* to return to the main menu.

When coders read and code a large number of cases, they unintentionally may begin to modify the meaning of the codes. This is known as coder drift—criteria used for the later cases drift from that used for the earlier cases. The more subjective the coding, the more likely this problem is to occur. In this example, coder drift is much more of a problem when coding sexual implications of the ad than when coding the gender of the advertiser. This is another reason for having detailed coding instructions that are often referred back to by the coder and for using multiple coders.

For the present, let's assume that the codings are reliable and do a preliminary test of our hypothesis that the content of the ads will differ by gender. Let's have the category "not stated" changed to "missing." *Press* the **F5** key. *Type* Y and *press <ENTER>*. Now *type* **NOT STATED** and *press <ENTER>* six times. In all subsequent analysis, cases coded NOT STATED on a variable will be assigned the missing data value on that variable.

Go to the **STATISTICAL ANALYSIS** menu and *select* **B. Tabular Statistics**. *Select* **3** as the row variable and **1** as the column variable. Use column percentaging.

```
Row Variable: 3) AGE-DES        Column Variable: 1) GENDER

                        MALE            FEMALE
UNDER 40                90.9             40.0
40 & OVER                9.1             60.0

V = 0.545
Prob. = 0.000
```

We can see that males are more likely to seek someone under 40 than are females. Remember, however, that we must consider the possibility of spurious relationships. Perhaps there is some other factor creating this relationship. An obvious possibility might be the age of the advertiser—perhaps the males are younger than the females, and when we control for the advertiser's age, there is no difference. Let's try this analysis. *Select* **3** as the row variable, **1** as the column variable, and **2** as the control variable:

```
Control variable: 2) AGE-AD: UNDER 40
Row Variable: 3) AGE-DES     Column Variable: 1) GENDER

                      MALE          FEMALE
UNDER 40             100.0           87.5
40 & OVER              0.0           12.5

n =                    20              8

V = 0.304
Prob. = 0.107
```

Press <ENTER> once to view the next category of the control variable.

```
Control variable: 2) AGE-AD: 40 & OVER
Row Variable: 3) AGE-DES     Column Variable: 1) GENDER

                      MALE          FEMALE
UNDER 40              90.0           20.0
40 & OVER            10.0           80.0

n =                    10             10

V = 0.704
Prob. = 0.000
```

Unfortunately, there are not enough cases to adequately test this alternative. The largest group, males under 40, has only 20 cases. The other groups have 10 or fewer. With only 100 cases, we are pretty much limited to examining bivariate relationships. If we were seriously interested in this issue, we would need to obtain a much larger sample of ads.

Your turn.

LIST OF ADVERTISERS

Use these cases and the code sheets on page 216 when doing Exercise 11, which begins on page 217.

Codes used by advertisers: LTR=Long Term Relationship C=Christian J=Jew W=White B=Black H=Hispanic A=Asian N/S=Non-smoker N/D=Non-drinker S=Single D=Divorced M=Male F=Female H/W=Height/weight D/D-free=Drugs and disease free P=Professional

1. CHRISTIAN AND KIND
SWM, 23, Christian values, 6'1", physically fit, attractive, enjoys summer activities, beaches, conversation. Would like to meet a Christian female for friendship, possibly more.

2. CHRISTIAN IN SEATTLE
Attractive, Christian SWM, 28, 6', H/W proportionate, active person, financially secure, stable and healthy. Would like to meet Christian female, for friendship, possibly more.

3. LOOKING FOR MS. RIGHT
SWM 23, 6'3", 165 lbs., brown/blue, enjoys camping, hiking, outdoors, movies, quiet nights. Seeking SF, 19–25, with similar interests. N/S, N/D.

4. A CUT ABOVE
Handsome, caring SWM, 47, 5'10", 190 lbs., honest, intelligent, business owner, enjoys arts, outdoors, travel. Seeking fit, classy lady, comfy in jeans/high heels, for LTR.

5. HARD-WORKING MAN
Handsome DWM, 40, 6'1", blond/blue, beard, country gentleman enjoys outdoors, camp fires, barbecues. Seeks attractive country girl, 35–45, N/S, light drinker for LTR.

6. BLACK GOLD
SBM, 37, 6'2", handsome, fit, romantic, easygoing, fun-loving, liberal, enjoys movies, sports, the arts, travel, dancing. Seeking lady with similar interests. 5'4"+ for LTR.

7. DON'T ANSWER THIS
Unless you seek a WM, 35, blonde/blue, who likes romantic nights and the outdoors. Please be WP/HF.

8. ROMANTIC TURK
Handsome, loving and passionate DWM, 46, 5'6", 140 lbs., willing to commit to a LTR, with active, fit, N/S lady 33–45, into personal and spiritual growth.

9. CARING KENT MAN
Thoughtful, caring SM, 39, 6', 185 lbs., brown/blue, enjoys motorcycles, music, movies, etc. Seeking SF, 21–38, H/W proportionate with similar interests, for possible LTR.

10. CHEF IN THE HOUSE
Attractive, Christian SBM, 30, N/S, N/D, easygoing, nice person, seeks very romantic, caring and honest SF friend, 25–33, N/S, N/D.

11. I COULD BE YOUR MAN
Are you 29–44, professional H/WF and have Christian values?

Professional, athletic DWM, 42, hazel eyes, 185 lbs., seeks woman to pamper and adore.

12. HIGH ENERGY WOMAN
Work/play hard? Me too. SWPM, 38, 5'10", slim, handsome. Not a homebody. Love R&B music, dancing, biking, talking, laughing, cuddling. Seeking SWPF 30–40.

13. TRUE MAN FOR FRIENDSHIP
Sensitive, intelligent, honest, handsome SWM, 40, 5'10", 160 lbs. Seeking partner to share life's pleasures. Attractive, proportionate, adventurous WF, 35–45. Emotionally available, monogamous LTR.

14. RENAISSANCE MAN
Handsome, Eastside WD/PCM, 45, business owner, 5'10", handsome, brown/blue, N/S, N/Drugs, athletic, enjoys outdoors, travel. Seeking pretty WPF, 5'2"–5'7", H/W proportionate for romance/LTR.

15. IN KEY
Attractive and active SWM, 34, 5'11", healthy, outdoors type, loves to cook and garden, honest and considerate, open-minded with common sense, enjoys talking.

16. AM I FOR YOU?
SWM, 38, 165 lbs., N/S, N/D, likes outdoors and indoors too. Seeking SF, 20–30.

17. SEEKING SOMEONE SPECIAL
SWM, 32, 5'10", 170 lbs., brown/hazel, enjoys walks, camping, and most outdoor activities. Seeking SWF, 28–35, with similar interests. Kids OK.

18. AVID ADVENTURER
Cute, rugged, strong SWM, 31, 5'11", 175 lbs., college-educated, financially independent, loves snowskiing, boating. Seeking slender woman of grace and sensuality, with inquisitive mind, who shares above interests. N/S, D/D-free.

19. GENUINE NICE GUY
N/S, attractive, DWPM, 34, seeks slender, attractive WPF, 25–40, who is honest and sincere, no games, for summer country concerts, weekend getaways, and romance.

20. WARM AND CARING
Active, athletic, DWPM, enjoys hiking, X-country skiing, dancing, tennis, and quiet times. Seeking similar energy level, female, 40–50, N/S, to share common interests now and into the future.

21. TALL, ATTRACTIVE, CELIBATE
SWM, 41, N/S, N/D, N/Drugs, seeks WF, N/S, 5'9"+, H/W proportionate for friendship and variety of activities; biking, skating, walks, talks, animals, dance, quiet times, possible LTR.

22. IN SEARCH OF
a best friend first. You: WF, H/W proportionate, attractive, pretty, sexy, 25–45. Kids ok. Me: a gentleman, WM, in 50s, ready for LTR.

23. FRIENDS FIRST
Handsome, fun SWM, 50, likes movies, dining out, outdoors. Seeks attractive SWF, 44–50, N/S, light drinker ok.

24. CHRISTIAN FRIEND
Let's be friends first. Native to Seattle. Likes scenic hiking, country fairs, swimming and adventure. I'm 44, never married, seeking attractive SWF, late 20s to early 40s. Let's meet over coffee.

25. BUSTING OUT OF MY SHELL
Sincere, honest good-looking SWM, 31, long dark hair, 5'11", 150 lbs., fit, likes movies, cats, music, creative ideas. Seeking attractive, slender female, 23–26.

26. SEEKING SOMEONE SPECIAL
SWM, 32, 6'1", 185 lbs., seeks SWF, 25–35, who wants to have fun and take a chance on enjoying life.

27. PERRY MASON UNDERSTUDY
Finds legal matters intriguing, king SWM, seeks compatible female, 45+, with humor. Mutual interests may include: piano music, art, horses, old houses.

28. LOOKING FOR LTR
Old-fashioned, romantic SWM, 23, 5'8", 140 lbs., brown/brown, enjoys bowling, golf, family and the beach. Seeking attractive, outgoing, SW/HF, 21–26, for friendship, possible LTR.

29. FUN-LOVING CHRISTIAN
Handsome, positive DWM, 35, 6'2", physically fit, creative and spontaneous. Seeking an attractive, fun-loving female, 25–36. Kids ok.

30. LONELY IN KENT
SWM, 26, seeks SF, 21–30, interested in outdoor activities, long walks and romantic evenings.

31. SEEKING OLDER WOMAN
Intelligent, good-looking SWM, 31, long hair, 5'10", in great shape, honest, creative. Seeking maturity of attractive, slim woman, 35–55, 130 lbs., who enjoys Christian and secular music, specifically heavy metal. Light drinker/smoker ok. Call me!

32. SUMMER ROMANCE
SWM, 41, 6', 175 lbs., brown/blue, wants summertime love with interesting lady. I have good sense of humor, very open, honest. Are you adventurous?

33. NEW TO WASHINGTON
SWM, 30, funny, open-minded and off-beat, not into looks, age or money. Seeking female companion for fun and romance.

34. LONELY AND SEARCHING
SHCM, 22, 5'5", 120 lbs., seeks SW/HCF, 18–21, with long brown hair, around 5'5" 139 lbs., who enjoys Christian and secular music, specifically heavy metal. Light drinker/smoker ok. Call me!

35. VERY HAIRY GUY
SM, 5'11", 215 lbs., long curly black hair, moustache and hairy body. N/D, N/S, likes mountains, movies, walks, rain. Seeking friendship with female, 35–47.

36. NEED TOUR GUIDE!
Attractive SWM, 32, financially secure. If you like intelligent conversation, dining out, and seek honesty and respect, I won't disappoint you! Seeking attractive, fun, responsible S/DF, 24–35.

37. SINGLE DAD
DWM, 43, 5'9", 185 lbs., loving father of two, handsome, enjoys camping, softball, boating, travel. You: S/DWF, 30–40, N/S, H/W proportionate, caring, honest, spontaneous.

38. TIMES A WASTIN'
DWPM, 30s, 5'10", H/W proportionate, loves the outdoors. Seeking marriage-minded lady, under 35, N/S, who likes children and appreciates family life and values.

39. RENTON MAN
SWM seeks D/DWF, 29–37, H/W proportionate, who enjoys movies, talking, going out, dinners, etc. N/Drugs, N/D. Smokers ok. Friendship first.

40. LAKESIDE LIVING
DWM, 37, 6'3", fit and trim, N/S, romantic gentleman, jeans or suit, needs compatible south-end type for life's adventures. Kids ok.

41. ROMANTIC COUNTRY BOY
Me: 22, brown/brown, H/W propor-
tionate. You: 22–30, blonde or brunette, H/W proportionate, likes C/W music. Seeking friend and romance for fun. No games.

42. BARBLESS IN SEATTLE
SWM, 39, 188 lbs., H/W proportionate, handsome, N/S, light drinker, loves fly fishing. Seeking SF, attractive, 22–39, H/W proportionate. Must also love fly fishing! Wants LTR!

43. CALL ME NOW
SWCM, 29, 5'10", 190 lbs., brown/brown, enjoys C&W music, movies, camping, sports. Looking for that one special woman to spend time with. N/S.

44. FRENCH MAN SEEKS AMOUR
SWM, 37, N/S, N/D, H/W proportionate, dark brown/green, seeks woman, 27–40, to travel and to explore with. Must be able to enjoy life.

45. SEEKING FUN AND YOU
DWM, 42, 6'3", medium build, enjoys fun, holding hands, walks, travel, camping, boating. Seeking light smoker/drinker. Pinochle a plus. LTR.

46. TOMBOYS AND SINGLE MOMS
Do you like the outdoors, art, tequila, rock music, boating, Mexican food, dancing, romance, adventure, laughter? SWM, 36, N/S, Mercer Island.

47. CLASSY, GQ GENTLEMAN
I'm 46, 5'10", trim, degreed, score an 8 out of 10, enjoy the finer things in life, honest, loving, gentle, and want to love a sweet, beautiful woman, 35–42.

48. ENDANGERED SPECIES . . .
committed father. WM, 43, 5'11", 220 lbs., seeks H/W proportionate mother, N/S, N/D, loves life and outdoors, most of all—complete and committed family life together. South King County.

49. TRUE BLUE CAMPER
SWM, 36, 5'8", 160 lbs., blonde/blue, enjoys hunting, camping, boating, light drinker/smoker. Seeking SWF, 28–40, H/W proportionate, for fun, romance, possible LTR.

50. EXTREMELY NICE GUY
Professional DWM, 47, 5'11", H/W proportionate, kind, considerate, likes drives, bike rides. I am a good catch. Seeking petite, professional female, 35–45, LTR.

51. COURT ME WITH ROMANCE
and experience the unforgettable, SWPF, 30, intoxicating elixir of sensuality and beauty, athletic, adventurous, seeks finely tuned, extraordinary SPM who can accommodate my passion for life.

52. COUNTRY GIRL/CITY STYLE
Cute, petite, DWPF, 37, non-Barbie, seeks tall, non-Ken, must love kids, animals, and fun. N/S, light drinker. Enjoys music, travel, warm nights, no couch potatoes.

53. AGE 22–27?
SCF, 21, pretty, enjoys outdoor activities. Seeking SM with a personality full of character, fun, and depth! Must be Christian, attractive, N/S, N/D.

54. BLONDE, BLUE-EYED
Educated DWF, enjoys beautiful music, dancing, outdoors, seeks DM gentleman, 45–55, who is kind, active, good conversationalist and happy.

55. HIGHLY EDUCATED BEAUTY
Tall, exciting, athletic, natural brunette seeks 4-year degreed (or more), charming business exec, 35–45, 6'+, interested in sports, the outdoors, cultural pursuits and a LTR.

56. ARTISTIC/ACTIVE/ ATTRACTIVE
Petite lady, 59 years young, looks 15+ years younger due to holistic lifestyle, seeks sensitive, secure soul mate, N/S, trim, fit gentleman of intelligence, awareness and sparkle.

57. BIG BEAUTIFUL SWF
Redhead seeks rugged, outdoor type, smoker ok, must like cuddling and dancing. Prefer over 5'11".

58. REDHEAD SWF SEEKS
sincere relationship with tall (6') SWM, enjoys camping, dancing and movies, who wants to have fun. Prefer N/S. N/Drugs, light drinker ok.

59. LOOKING FOR WHAT?
Let's look together. DWF, 50, 5'1", H/W proportionate, N/S, light drinker, family-oriented, likes having fun doing almost anything. Let's have coffee, talk, see what follows, maybe just friends.

60. LIFE WOULD BE COMPLETE
if I had the special someone to share it with. SWF, 35, blonde/blue, H/W proportionate, easy on the eyes, adventurous, passionate, playful, searching for a man that is open-minded and into sharing and caring as I am.

61. QUEEN SIZE
SWF, 27, seeks king size SWM, with good heart. Are you tired of being overlooked because of your weight? Me too, let's talk. Don't be shy!

62. GOLF ANYONE?
Outgoing, classy, athletic. Eastside DWPF, 44, brunette, H/W proportionate, financially secure, loves golf, biking, skiing, theater, fine dining, good conversation. Seeking professional counterpart, 38–48.

63. PRECIOUS JEM
JF, 40, 5'7", 180 lbs., brown/brown, sensual, sensitive, stubborn, enjoys crafts, country living, hobbies, traveling, seek SCM gentle-spirited, 35–43 with similar characteristics for friendship/LTR.

64. PASSIONATE AND STYLISH
Sensual intelligence, sublime touch, and the rhythm of the blues. All with significant sophistication at 31, for an appreciative professional over 45.

65. OLD-FASHIONED LOVE
DWF, 45, N/S, seeks LTR/possible marriage with professional M, with intelligence, integrity, humor, class. Only those commitment-minded please apply.

66. SMART, PERKY WITH ZEST
SWF, H/W proportionate, attractive, east and west coast person, with zest for life, likes boating, outdoor activities, every day is a joy. Seeking professional gentleman, 50s, with same ideas/values.

67. SEEKING A SPECIAL FRIEND
SWF, 47, H/W proportionate, enjoys fishing, camping, outdoors, animals, C/W. Seeking one-woman man, 43–55, light smoker/drinker ok, for friendship first, possible LTR later.

68. A FANTASY?
SWF, 43, 5'6", H/W proportionate, financially secure, active, enjoys life. Seeking SWM, 40–55, H/W proportionate, fit, financially secure, who can dance, N/S, light drinker, disease-free.

69. LEGS, LEGS, LEGS
SWPF, 30, 6'2", slender, looking for you . . . SWM, 28–40, N/S, who likes country music, dinners out, movies, picnics, and finding the humor in life.

70. SEEKING ROMANTIC COMPANION
DWF, 45, pretty, H/W proportionate, 5'4", N/S, light drinker, enjoys soccer, movies, cooking, cuddling, seeks SWM, 40–50, 5'10"+, attractive, fun-loving, H/W proportionate, sincere.

71. SPIRITUALLY-MINDED
SJPF, 42, pretty, with fun sense of humor, varied interests, H/W proportionate, N/S, light drinker, would like to get to know genuine male 40–48, under 6' for LTR. No games.

72. I'M A BRAT!
SWF, 29, wants to play. Love to
camp, golf, bike, travel. Seeking
SWM, 27–45, who is financially
secure, N/S, can keep with my quick
wit. No geeks.

73. LIFE'S BEST WHEN SHARED
Beautiful brunette, New Yorker CEO,
35, 5'4", 105 lbs., caring, intelligent,
Kosher, seeks handsome, successful,
educated, traditional JM, with strong
values; kind, generous, loving.

74. I'M LOST—FIND ME!
DWF, 30, loves sun, dancing,
romance, flexible—I'll follow your
lead. If you're fit and built like Van
Damme, you're my man. No geeks.

75. EASTSIDE CLASSY
Passionate, 39-year-old SWPF, enjoys
outdoors, very fit and versatile.
Seeking N/S, light drinking, tall, sincere and financially secure WPM for
LTR. I'm 5'10", blondish/blue, slender, romantic, pretty, fun!

76. ROCKY MOUNTAIN HIGH
High-energy, attractive SWF, H/W
proportionate, professional with passion for conversation, cuddling, sail-
ing, skiing, boating, bicycling, travel
and tenderness. Seeking SWM, 55+,
H/W proportionate, N/S.

77. R U MAN ENOUGH?
DWF, 38, 5'11", H/W proportionate,
enjoys biking, gardening, travel and
darts. Seeking tall S/DWM
employed, clean-cut, for LTR. Light
smoker/drinker, D/D-free.

78. BORN COUNTRY
A heart full of love, a genuine friend,
a happy lady! DWCF, N/S, N/D.
Very active, secure, slender, young 53.

79. SUMMER FUN
Attractive WF, 39, 5'10", blonde,
devoted part-time mom, seeks tall,
Eastside gentleman. We're athletic,
educated, healthy, N/S, desire LTR,
with romance.

80. RSVP ASAP
SWF, 25, easygoing, secure, professional, enjoys boating, scuba diving
and traveling. Seeks SWM, 25–35,
stable, attractive and financially
secure.

81. KIND & COMPASSIONATE
Petite, attractive, SWPF, early 50s,
seeks soulmate for LTR. I'm active,
spiritual and enjoy outdoor activities, movies, bookstores, travel, animals, and many other interests.

82. TAKE A CHANCE
Very attractive SWF, mid-30s, 5'6",
H/W proportionate, blonde/blue,
educated, outgoing, introspective,
caring, sensual. Seeking same in fun,
attractive male, 35–40, 5'10"+, 200 lbs.
for possible LTR. N/S, light drinker.

83. CUTE, SWEET & PETITE
Attractive DWF, 43, 5'2", 115 lbs.,
long light-brown/green, enjoys boating, hiking, walks on beach, trying
new things. Seeking someone special
36–47, 5'9"–6'2", physically fit, secure
for monogamous LTR.

84. COUNTRY RAISED
SWCF, H/W proportionate, 5'6", 160

lbs., country, lives in city. Seeking
SWCM, 40–48.

85. TOTALLY UNIQUE
This SWF, 42, attractive, bright, educated, unpretentious, enjoys country
living, nature, walks, animals, gardening, reading, relaxing. Seeking
SWM, similar age and interests, for
LTR.

86. BLUE JEANS & MINK
DWCF, 5'7", 130 lbs., fit, attractive,
family-oriented, spiritually/emotion-
ally strong with varied interests:
Mozart to camping, etc. Seeking honest WPM, 40–48 for LTR.

87. ATTRACTIVE BROWN-EYED
GIRL
This 40-year-old, H/W proportionate
N/S is looking for my best friend,
who wants LTR. Must be confident,
loyal, honest, emotionally/financial-
ly together, with Christian values.
Please call. N/S only.

88. CRITIQUE THIS
SWF, 27, outgoing, spontaneous, professional, enjoys boating, jeeping,
island hopping. Seeks SWM, 27–37,
attractive, confident, financially
secure, adventurous, with similar
likes.

89. SMILING EYES
Attractive DWF, 47, N/S, light
drinker, N/Drugs, outgoing, affectionate, kind, spontaneous, positive,
active, professional seeks SWM,
43–50, H/W proportionate 6', with
similar values and morals. Loves
nature.

90. ROSES ARE RED
Violets are blue. I'm sick of the dating scene, how about you? SWF, 27, sick of game players, losers. Seeking LTR with professional SWM 27–35.

91. FASHIONABLY LATE
SWF, 39, 5'7", athletic, attractive, seeks one special man, intelligent, 6'+, successful, adventurous. Looking for somebody special.

92. WARM, COZY LIFE
DWF, 59, has happy, affectionate, tasteful lifestyle to share with sturdy, appreciative, educated man. Honesty, humor, communication, compassion a must for both. Eastside, Seattle, NS.

93. ENERGETIC
Sophisticated, educated lady, likes outdoors, ethnic activities, sunshine, flowers, life in general. Life's too full for movies or TV. Seeking SWM, 45–55, 5'10"+.

94. LIFE IS GOOD . . .
and getting better! Widowed WF, 53, enjoys family/friends, home/garden, travel/walks. Seeking articulate, metaphysical, romantic SWPM, N/S, light drinker. N/Drugs. Leave your message.

95. ALONE
Attractive DWF, 50+, wants companion/friendship with spontaneous, adventurous S/DWM, 55–60, 5'10"+, N/S, light drinker, with good sense of humor, enjoys outdoors and travel.

96. CUTE, FUN AND JUST ME
Honest, fun-loving, brown/brown, 33, 5'4", H/W proportionate, D/D-

free, N/S, light drinker, seeks same in Harrison Ford/Tom Hanks type to share life's pleasures.

97. PETITE BLONDE
Successful, professional DWF, 44, Christian, N/S, light drinker, "loves water & sun," pretty smile, 5'3", 110 lbs., seeks successful man who loves children and family for fun, romance, LTR.

98. WILL PAINT YOUR WAGON
Scintillating artist, 60s beauty. WPF, stylish fun, gourmet cook, desire savvy SWP "He-man," 55–65, 5'9", N/S, fun loving companionship/life adventures.

99. CARING AND HAPPY
DWF, 54, 5'6", N/S, height/weight proportionate, enjoys golf, movies, dancing, sports. Happy with life, like to meet man with similar interests. Let's meet for coffee.

100. SEEKING PRINCE CHARMING
42 year-old mother (of three boys), 5'2", long blonde/brilliant blue, well-educated, active, altruistic. You? Fun, adventurous, secure, no hang-ups. Integrity, affection, kindness and prayers are musts.

CODE SHEET FOR CODING NEW VARIABLES

Case	AGE-AD1	LTR1	Case	AGE-AD1	LTR1
1			26		
2			27		
3			28		
4			29		
5			30		
6			31		
7			32		
8			33		
9			34		
10			35		
11			36		
12			37		
13			38		
14			39		
15			40		
16			41		
17			42		
18			43		
19			44		
20			45		
21			46		
22			47		
23			48		
24			49		
25			50		

This worksheet section continues to use the **CONTENT** data file. If you did not immediately continue from the previous section, you will need to open the file and set the "not stated" category to missing data. To do this, *press* the **F5** key. *Type* **Y** and *press* <ENTER>. Then *type* **NOT STATED** and *press* <ENTER> *six times.*

1. Ideally, all variables on all cases would be coded at least twice. However, this type of coding takes considerable time. To understand the process, you will code (enter data for) the *first 50* cases on just two variables: 11) AGE-AD1 and 13) LTR1. Using the **F3** key, look at the special notes on each of these variables before beginning your coding. You may use the code sheet on the preceding page to code the cases, or you may code the data directly into the MicroCase data file.

    a. After you have finished the coding, use tabular statistics to look at the relationship between **2) AGE-AD** and **11) AGE-AD1**.

    How many cases have been coded the same on both variables?

    _____

    What is the value of V?   _____

    Based on this information, do you think **2) AGE-AD** is reliable enough to be used in analysis? (Circle one.)   Yes   No

    b. Now look at the relationship between **4) LTR** and **13) LTR1**.

    How many cases have been coded the same on both variables?

    _____

    What is the value of V?   _____

    Based on this information, do you think **4) LTR** is reliable enough to be used in analysis? (Circle one.)   Yes   No

2. When a range is given rather than an age, the younger end is used in the coding. What other technique(s) could be used for coding the age when a range is given? Discuss the relative advantages and disadvantages of these approaches.

3. Test the hypothesis that the physical attractiveness of the desired respondent will be more important in ads placed by males than in those placed by females.

	MALE	FEMALE
NONE		
MINIMAL		
STRESSED		

$V =$ _____

Prob. = _____

What is your conclusion?

4. Test the hypothesis that financial security of the desired respondent will be more important in ads placed by females than in those placed by males.

	MALE	FEMALE
STATED		
NONE IND.		

V = _____

Prob. = _____

What is your conclusion?

5. Test the hypothesis that an interest in long-term relationships is more likely to be expressed in ads by females than in ads by males. Please show your analysis.

	MALE	FEMALE
LTR		
?		
NO		

V = _____

Prob. = _____

What is your conclusion?

6. Test the hypothesis that an interest in long-term relationships is affected by the age of the advertiser.

	UNDER 40	40 & OVER
LTR		
?		
NO		

V = _____

Prob. = _____

What is your conclusion?

Projects

With your Student MicroCase, you can create a file with up to 15 variables for as many as 100 cases. While you can create only one such file at a time, you can create new files as many times as you want—each new file simply replaces the old file. Further, you can add up to 15 variables to the **USA** file. If you do any of the projects described later, you will need to set up such a file.

Let's use a very small set of hypothetical data to demonstrate how to create a MicroCase file and enter data. We will use just three variables for just five cases, but the same procedures would be used if you were creating a data file with hundreds of variables and thousands of cases. Suppose we have the following variables for five cities:

City Identification Number	Political Party Affiliation of the Mayor	Median Education Level
Jones City = 1	Democrat = 1	12.5
Smithville = 2	Republican = 2	13.6
Brownsberg = 3	Democrat = 1	11.8
Crossroads = 4	—	12.9
Westville = 5	Republican = 2	12.7

Note that we already have coded the city variable by assigning identification numbers and that we have coded the mayors' political party affiliations as 1 for Democrat and 2 for Republican. We do not have any data for the political party affiliation of the mayor of Crossroads—thus, this case will be missing for this variable. We do not need to assign codes to median education level because this variable already consists of numbers.

We go through three steps in order to create a new MicroCase data file and enter the data: creating the file, defining the variables that will be included in the file, and entering the actual data for those variables. Let's go through these steps for the city data.

STEP 1: CREATE A NEW DATA FILE

On the **DATA AND FILE MANAGEMENT** menu, **select J. Create New Data File**. (NOTE: If you have previously created a file, then you will get a message that says a student-created file already exists, and you will be asked whether you wish to erase it. In order to replace the old file with a new one, *type* **Y** (for Yes) and *press <ENTER>*.)

The program then asks for a name for the file. Type in a descriptive name consisting of 1–8 characters. In this example, *type* **CITIES** and *press <ENTER>*. The program asks for a description of the file. This description can be up to 78 characters long. Here *type* the following and then *press <ENTER>*: **Selected Variables for Five Cities**.

The program then asks for the number of cases. In this situation, we are using data for 5 cities. So *type* **5** and *press <ENTER>*. At this point, the program returns you to the **DATA AND FILE MANAGEMENT** menu, and you're ready for the next stage: defining the variables. (NOTE: If you are using the *full version* of MicroCase, before the program returns to the main menu, you will be asked to enter a code for missing data. Just *press <ENTER>* to accept the default –9999.)

STEP 2: DEFINE THE VARIABLES

In this step, you will give the MicroCase system information about each variable. *Press* the letter **A** for **Define Variables/Recodes**. The program will respond that there are zero variables in the data set so far, and it will state **Variable Number: 1**. *Press <ENTER>* to begin defining variable number 1.

The program asks for a **name** for the variable. *A variable name contains from 1 to 10 characters, including any blank spaces in it.* The name should give you a quick idea of what the variable is. For the first variable, we will give each city a case identification number—1 for the first city, 2 for the second city, and so on up to 5 for the last city. Let's call this variable **CITY ID**. So *type* **CITY ID** and *press <ENTER>*.

The program now asks for a **description** of the variable. *A variable description can be up to 800 spaces long.* You type in a variable description *without pressing <ENTER> at the end of the line* if there is more than one line. When you press <ENTER> this ends the variable description and goes to the next step. For this particular variable, just *type* **City identification number** and *press <ENTER>*.

The program now asks for the **type of variable**. We will assign each city an integer (whole) number. So *type* the letter **I** (for Integer) and *press <ENTER>*.

The program now asks for the **lowest possible value** for this variable—and, in the next step, it will ask for the **highest possible value**. This helps to avoid errors when you enter data, because, if you type in a value outside the possible range, the program will alert you. For this **CITY ID** variable, we will assign the first city the number 1 and the last city the number 5. Thus, for the low value, *type* **1** and *press <ENTER>*. The program asks for the highest possible value. *Type* **5** and *press <ENTER>*.

Next the program asks whether the preceding information is correct. Look over the information you have entered so far to make sure it is right. If everything is correct, just *press <ENTER>* to accept the default Y for Yes. If there are errors, *type* **N** (for No) and the program will take you back to the beginning to let you correct any mistakes. If you go back to correct mistakes, redo any part that is not correct and just *press <ENTER>* for any part that is already correct.

The program now asks whether you wish to **label categories**. In this particular situation, the variable will consist of a number for each city and really does not require any labels. However, let's label the five numbers using the names of the cities. So *press <ENTER>* to accept the default Y for Yes response.

For the number 1, *type* the first city's name—**Jones City**—and *press <ENTER>*. For the number 2, *type* the second city's name—**Smithville**—and *press <ENTER>*. Continue until you have typed in all five cities' names. (NOTE: A label for a category of a variable can be anywhere from 1 to 10 spaces long.)

The program asks whether the labels are correct. If they are correct, simply *press <ENTER>*. If they are not correct, *type* **N** and *press <ENTER>*, and the program will let you go back to correct any errors—you use the **arrow** keys to move up and down and back and forth in the set of labels.

The program is now ready for you to define variable number 2. The screen reads **Variable Number: 2**. *Press <ENTER>* to begin defining variable 2. The second variable is the political party affiliation of the mayor of the city. Let's call this variable **PARTY**. So, *type* **PARTY** and *press <ENTER>*. For the variable description, *type* **Mayor's Political Party Affiliation** and *press <ENTER>*.

We coded this variable as 1 for *Democrat* and 2 for *Republican*. Thus, we have integer numbers again. So *type* **I** (for Integer) and *press <ENTER>*. Next *type* the number **1** for the low value and *press <ENTER>*. Then *type* **2** for the high value and *press <ENTER>*. Check to make sure that the information is correct. If so, *press <ENTER>*.

Press <ENTER> again to label the categories. For the number 1, *type* **Democrat** and *press <ENTER>*. For the number 2, *type* **Republican** and *press <ENTER>*. Check to make sure the labels are correct. If so, *press <ENTER>*. If not, *type* **N** so that you can correct any errors.

Press <ENTER> again to begin defining variable number 3. *Type* **MED EDUC** (for median education level) and *press <ENTER>*. For the variable description, *type* **Median Education Level for the City** and *press <ENTER>*.

Unlike the previous variables, this is not an integer variable—it has a decimal in it. So *type* **D** (for Decimal) and *press <ENTER>*. There is one digit to the right of the decimal (e.g., 12.3). Therefore, in response to the question about the number of digits to the right of the decimal, *type* **1** and *press <ENTER>*.

For just a few cases like this, we can easily see the low and high values. However, if we had a number of cases, it might be inconvenient to figure out the low and high values for a decimal variable. For decimal variables, however, we can omit the low and high values. Therefore, *press <ENTER> twice* to skip these two questions.

Press <ENTER> again if the information is correct. Note that the program did not ask whether we wanted to label the categories. Decimal variables are set up in terms of real numbers—not categories.

The program is now ready for us to define variable number 4, but there isn't any variable number 4. So, *press <ENTER> twice* and you will be returned to the **DATA AND FILE MANAGEMENT** menu.

STEP 3: ENTERING THE DATA

You are now ready to type in the actual data. *Select* **C. Enter Data from Keyboard**. The program then gives you a choice of entering data by row or by column or by questionnaire. We usually enter data by row. So, *type* the number **1** for row and *press <ENTER>*.

The program then asks whether you want to enter new data, edit existing data, or do rekey verification. In this situation, you want to enter new data, so *press* the number **1** and *press <ENTER>*. However, while you're here, note that, if you wanted to *correct* data that you had already entered, you would select the **edit existing data** option.

NOTE: If you use questionnaire data entry, you will be asked if you wish to use the "no answer" category. If you choose not to use this option, then the respondent must answer each question—it is not possible to skip a question. This is the option preferred by most researchers. Missing data options, such as "refused," "not applicable," and "don't know," are provided as possible answers and the respondent is forced to select one of the available categories. If, however, you choose to include the "no answer" category, the respondent will be given "no answer" as the last category on each question.

The program will then ask for the list of cases for which you will be entering data. In this situation, you will be entering data for all five cases. Simply *press <ENTER>* to accept the default—*all* cases. Note, however, that there are situations (e.g., large data files) in which people cannot enter all the data for all the cases at one sitting. The MicroCase analysis system allows you to enter data for some cases and then come back later to finish entering data for the rest of the cases.

Similarly, the program now asks for the list of variables for which you will be entering data. *Press <ENTER>* to accept the default—*all* variables. Again, however, note that you could enter data for just certain variables at one point and then enter the rest of the data at some later time. Make sure the information so far is correct and then *press <ENTER>*. The screen will now look like this:

CITY ID   PARTY   MED EDUC

1   —

The blinking cursor is on the row marked 1 (for the first case) and under the first variable (**CITY ID**). The program is ready to receive data for the first case for the first variable. *Type* **1** (for city number 1—Jones City) and *press <ENTER>*. The cursor now moves to the second variable (**PARTY**) for the first case. For the variable **PARTY**, *type* **1** for Democrat and *press <ENTER>*. For the variable **MED EDUC**, *type* **12.5** and *press <ENTER>*.

Now you are ready to enter data for the second case (Smithville). Following the steps above, go ahead and enter data for all the cases. Before you do that, however, please note two things.

First, if you have *missing data* for a case for a variable—such as the political party affiliation of the mayor of Crossroads—you simply press <ENTER> to skip it. When you do this, MicroCase will beep just in case you accidentally skipped an entry. Then MicroCase will assign the missing value to this case for this variable—and exclude this case from the analysis of this particular variable.

Second, if you make a mistake in data entry, you can back up one entry at a time by pressing both the **Shift** and the **Tab** keys at the same time. To move forward again, just press <ENTER>.

After you have entered the last variable for the last case, the program will ask whether you are finished. Simply *press <ENTER>* and the program will return you to the main menu. You have now set up a MicroCase data file from start to finish.

How to Stop Entering Data and Continue Later

Suppose you cannot finish entering all the data at one time. How do you stop without losing your work?

1. Make a note about where—which case—you entered last. You need to know this when you start up again. Do not stop in the middle of a case.
2. *Press* the escape key, the key marked **ESC**.
3. The program asks if you want to escape. *Type* **Y** (for Yes) and *press <ENTER>*.
4. You will be given a choice. Just *press <ENTER>* to save your data and exit.
5. You will be returned to the menu, and you can now exit the program.

How do you start up again later when you are ready to complete the data entry?

1. Start MicroCase, *open* the data file, and go to the **DATA AND FILE MAN-AGEMENT** menu.

2. *Type* C for **Enter Data from Keyboard**.
3. *Type* the number **1** to enter data by row.
4. *Type* the number **1** again to enter new data.
5. The screen tells you how many cases and variables are in the data set. It also asks you to provide the list of cases for which you will be entering data. Check your notes to see what the number of the last case you entered was. Then indicate the list of cases for which you will enter data. For example, let's say that you had already entered data in a file for three cases and you are now ready to enter data for cases 4 and 5. You would *type* **4–5** and *press <ENTER>*.
6. *Press <ENTER> two more times* to accept the default (all) for the variables to be entered and to verify that the information is correct.
7. You are now ready to continue entering the data.

FINDING ERRORS IN A DATA FILE

MicroCase includes an option that lists the values of variables by case, and you can use this procedure to compare the data in your file against the original data in order to find any errors. Let's go through this process with the **CITIES** data file.

With the **CITIES** file open, *select* **D. List or Print Variable Values** from the **DATA AND FILE MANAGEMENT** menu. The program asks whether you want to list the data on the screen or print it. For present purposes, let's list the data on the screen. So, *type* **1** and *press <ENTER>*. *Press <ENTER> three more times* to step through the options and list the data on the screen. As you go through this process, note that you could easily obtain lists for just selected variables or selected cases.

At this point, the data are listed. However, if you were looking at a large data file, the entire list of data would not be visible on the screen at one time. For larger data files, you move around the list with the following keys. Use the **Tab** key to move to the right—each time you press the **Tab** key, it moves the cursor one variable to the right. Use the **Shift/Tab** combination of keys to move to the left. When you hold down the **Shift** key and press the **Tab** key, the cursor moves one variable to the left. Use the **Page Up** and **Page Down** keys and the **up** and **down arrow** keys to move the cases up and down.

Check the data in your file against the original data. This can be done best if one person reads from the screen while another person checks the original data. Make notes—including the case and the variable—about any errors you find. When you are finished checking the data, *press <ENTER>* to return to the **DATA AND FILE MANAGEMENT** menu.

CORRECTING ERRORS IN THE DATA FILE

You should have a list of errors so that you know *which variables* for *which cases* need to be corrected. Assuming you have a list, let's go through this process for correcting errors.

1. From the **DATA AND FILE MANAGEMENT** menu, *type* **C** for **Enter Data from Keyboard**.
2. *Type* the number **1** to select the row option and *press <ENTER>*.
3. *Type* the number **2** and *press <ENTER>* to select the **Edit existing data** option.
4. The program will respond that there are five cases and three variables in the data set, and it will ask for a list of cases for which you will be entering data. *Type* in the numbers (the **CITY ID** numbers) of all the cases for which you need to correct data, and then *press <ENTER>*. NOTE: List the cases separated by commas: 1, 3, 5.
5. The program will ask for the list of variables. List all variables for which corrections need to be made. NOTE: List the variables separated by commas. *Example:* 1, 3, 5.
6. The program will ask whether the information is correct. If it is, *press <ENTER>*.
7. The program will present the data entry for the first variable for the first case you said needed corrections. If this entry is not correct, *correct it* and then *press <ENTER>*. If the entry is correct, just *press <ENTER>*.
8. The program will present the data entry for the next variable for the first case you said needed corrections. If the entry is already correct, just *press <ENTER>*. Otherwise, *correct it* and then *press <ENTER>*.
9. This process will continue until all data entries for all the cases and variables you specified have been checked. After the last entry has been checked, the program will ask whether you are finished. If the data entries are correct, *press <ENTER>*.

HUMAN SUBJECTS GUIDELINES

You have probably read about the medical experiment in which men with syphilis were denied penicillin, a known cure, in the quest for additional scientific information. Or the studies of the effect of radiation on individuals who were not informed of the potential risks. While the actual research studies in these incidents undoubtedly are more ambiguous ethically than these headlines suggest, the fact remains that until relatively recently, the ethical treatment of subjects in research was left almost exclusively to the judgment of the researcher. In the 1970s, to protect the public from unethical research, granting agencies started to require that all research must stay within a set of ethical guidelines. To guarantee conformity, each research proposal must be approved by a special committee. Today, virtually all universities and granting organizations require a *human subjects* review for proposed research in which the subjects or participants are humans. (Incidentally, these procedures also protect researchers from lawsuits by unethical subjects.)

Educational projects, such as those suggested in this section, are generally exempt from this process unless the results of the research will be published. Your instructor will inform you if you will need any special clearance before proceeding with an assigned project.

If, at some future time, you wish to conduct your own research, you should review the ethical concerns described in the text for your particular research approach. In addition, you should design your research project using the following suggestions:

- If possible, obtain the informed, voluntary consent of subjects in research. If it is not feasible to obtain consent in advance of the research, then try to obtain consent afterward.

- If there is even a modest degree of risk of harm to the subjects, then it is mandatory that you obtain the informed, voluntary consent of subjects prior to the research.

- Minimize any risk of harm to research participants which might result from the research in any way—from the initial stages of the research to any problems that might occur in the aftermath of the publication of results.

- Take whatever steps are necessary to protect the identity of research participants (e.g., destroying information that might identify participants, disguising the location where the research took place, and presenting results of the study in such a way that no individuals can be identified).

- Do not deceive the subject unless it is the only feasible way to achieve the research objective and adequate provisions have been made to protect the subject from harm.

- Protect the privacy and dignity of the participants.
- When subjects have been used in experimental research, detect and remove any harmful consequences to the subject (e.g., stress).

You may also want to consider the following three aspects which come under particularly close scrutiny during evaluation of the use of human subjects in social science:

1. INVASION OF PRIVACY

This is probably the most common ethical problem in social science research. Before collecting any data, social researchers must inform each participant who will have access to the information and how the information will be used. Steps must then be taken to maintain the promised degree of privacy. This is primarily an issue in survey research, and the text discusses several methods used to maintain the confidentiality of such information. In field research, you must also be careful to protect the privacy of those observed.

When illegal or criminal behavior is studied, the researcher has an additional burden. Social scientists, like newspaper reporters and unlike doctors and lawyers, have no right of confidentiality regarding information and sources. If a list of survey respondents or a tape recording is subpoenaed by a court, a researcher may be held in contempt and punished for refusing to produce the information. In such studies, the researcher should not promise a greater degree of confidentiality than is legally possible. A related problem occurs if the researcher uncovers evidence of continuing criminal activity. For example, a field researcher may find that a particular gang burns buildings on a regular basis and may even have knowledge of future crimes. Failure to report this information could lead to criminal charges against the researcher.

2. STUDIES INVOLVING DECEPTION

In some studies, subjects or participants may not be told the complete truth. This is most common in experimental studies. For example, the experiment described in the text involves a deception: Subjects are led to believe they are listening to other participants when in fact they are listening to a tape recording and, moreover, the taped conversation encourages them to believe that another participant has suffered a seizure. Other types of research may also involve some level of deception. Field researchers may sometimes imply they hold a position when, in fact, they do not. For example, in observing a hospital, a researcher may dress as an orderly, a nurse, or a doctor to be less obtrusive. Even survey researchers may sometimes wish to conceal the exact purpose of their survey.

Deception is a touchy ethical issue. If the same information can be obtained without deception, this is almost always preferable. Most human-subjects committees will weigh the degree and effect of the deception against the potential gain of the study. If deception is used, subjects must be *debriefed* after the study to minimize any consequences of the deception. For example, in the experiment described above, subjects who did not leave the room to seek help may later worry and feel guilty about their behavior. The researchers are responsible for discussing the actual study with subjects so that these feelings do not occur. Unfortunately, no amount of debriefing can erase the subject's knowledge of how he or she behaved in the particular circumstances.

3. INFORMED CONSENT AND COERCION

Participants and subjects in studies must be informed of the purpose of the study and must be allowed the opportunity to refuse to participate. For example, an instructor cannot *require* any student in a class to complete a questionnaire for a research project—such participation must be voluntary.

When adequate information is provided, most social science research projects are readily approved by the relevant committees.

PROJECT 1: DOING A SURVEY

In this project, you can learn something about students at your college or university. Before you begin, decide on the purpose of your survey. Perhaps you want to see if males and females at your school exhibit gender stereotypes. Or you might want to see if there are sex differences in deviance: Are males more likely to have been picked up by the police than are females? You could determine if students at your school are well informed on certain demographic facts, such as, what the world population is. You could see to what extent students' political views match those of their parents. You could even replicate the methodological experiment described in Exercise 10.

After you have selected your topic, design your questionnaire. A variety of possible questions is listed in Appendix A, or you can design your own questions. In the student version of MicroCase, a data file is limited to 15 variables, so you may ask a maximum of 15 questions.

After you have developed your questionnaire, construct your analysis plan. Which questions will be independent variables and which will be dependent variables? What analysis will you use to answer your research question? Are there possible sources of spuriousness to consider? Any potential intervening variables? It is extremely important to develop your analysis plan before finalizing the questionnaire. This is the only way you can be sure to collect data on all relevant variables. **Warning**: Even very experienced professional researchers have made ridiculous errors of omission in their surveys. For example, a multimillion-dollar longitudinal study of education, following people from ages 16 through 26, failed to ever ask whether respondents had completed college. So, after you are sure you have included everything you will need to know, check again.

You will need to decide whether you will use phone interviews, face-to-face interviews, or mailed questionnaires. If you plan to conduct phone interviews, compose your opening statement. For example, you might say the following:

Hello, this is _____. I'm a social science student at _____.
As a class project, I'm conducting interviews with a sample of students.
Could you spare five minutes to answer some questions?

If you are going to do face-to-face interviews, you will want to work out your approach, perhaps adapting the opening phone statement. If you are going to mail the surveys, you will need to write an appropriate cover letter.

You can now pretest the survey on two or three friends. If necessary, rework the questionnaire. Again review your analysis plan to make sure that you have all relevant information.

Now you can select your sample. Obtain a list of phone numbers or addresses for all students (or perhaps all undergraduates) at your college or university, and randomly select a sample of 50 students. You can then proceed to collect the data.

After the data have been collected, create your MicroCase data set. Enter the data from the questionnaires. Complete your planned analysis and write up the results.

PROJECT 2: DOING A COMPARATIVE STUDY

1. In this project, you'll use information from the *Census of Retail Trade* to test ideas about the effect of the age profiles on retail trade. Before you begin, make sure that you have access to the *Census of Retail Trade*. You may want to examine these reports to get an idea of the type of information available.

Develop two hypotheses about the effect of the age distribution on the consumption of products and services, using states as the units of analysis. For example, you might speculate that states with a high percentage of children will have a higher ratio of spending in grocery stores to spending in restaurants.

After you have developed your hypotheses, you will need to find data on the variables. The age distribution is available from many sources—the *Statistical Abstract of the United States* is probably the most convenient. If necessary, convert this number to a rate, that is, from the number of children under 12 to the percent of the population under 12. You can obtain the measures of the dependent variables from the *Census of Retail Trade*. Again convert these to rates.

You may now enter the data into the **USA** data file—just add these variables to the end of the data file. (Refer to *How to Create a MicroCase File and Enter Data* at the beginning of this section, but start with task A: Define Variables/Recodes, since you are adding variables to a file that already has been created.) Test your hypotheses and write up your results.

2. Create a MicroCase data file of the 25 largest nations. (Refer to *How to Create a MicroCase File and Enter Data* at the beginning of this section.) You will first have to determine which nations should be included. You may obtain population figures for each nation from the *Statistical Abstract of the United States*. Develop a hypothesis that can be tested with this data set. For example, you might speculate that the higher the per capita income, the lower the birth rate.

Find appropriate data for each country. Convert the numbers to rates if necessary. Enter the data into your MicroCase data file and test your hypothesis. Write up your results.

PROJECT 3: DOING A FIELD STUDY

Two suggested projects are described here. Since you are observing in public places, you need not obtain permission from those individuals you will observe. However, you will probably want to appear as a "natural" element of the setting. If people know you are taking notes on their behavior, they may not only change the behavior, but also confront you or file a complaint about you. An easy guise for a college student is to pretend to be studying: some reading, some writing, and much thoughtful gazing into space.

When you organize your notes and write your report, develop a central theme. What did you find most interesting? Use your observations to support your interpretation of events.

1. Observe children on playground equipment on several different days. Before you start taking notes, you will want to think about the types of questions you might be able to answer. Which pieces of equipment are most popular? Are these preferences affected by the age or sex of the children? Do children play in groups or by themselves? Are there any age or sex differences in group play? Are there pieces of equipment that encourage cooperation or promote competition among the children? Does the play tend to be segregated by age and sex? Are adults present? To what extent do the adults control the children's behavior? Are some children more popular than others? Are there any "outcasts"? If so, can you determine why this happens?

Remember that adults lurking around playgrounds could appear suspicious. If you plan to observe at a school playground, obtain permission from the principal in advance. You might ask the principal to sign a letter that you have prepared so that you have proper "credentials." If you are observing at a public park, you might want to have a letter from your professor on your college stationery.

2. Observe a fast-food restaurant at different times on different days. As a good field researcher, you should obtain permission from the manager or owner before beginning your observations. If you plan to observe the staff, ask the manager not to reveal your role. As a courtesy, try not to occupy a table when customers need it. If necessary, limit your observations to times when the restaurant is less crowded.

You might choose to observe either the staff or the customers or both. What is the age and sex composition of the staff? Who's in charge? Does informal staff interaction appear to be a function of personal characteristics or of their role in the restaurant? Do there appear to be any conflicts among the staff? If there are, how are these conflicts resolved? Do the staff talk with customers or just fill their orders? What is the attitude of the staff? How do they react when inundated with customers? What do they do when there are no customers?

How does the customer base change over time and over the days of the week? How do individuals who eat by themselves behave? Do they ignore others, perhaps reading newspapers or books, or do they try to engage others in conversation? Are there any sex, age, or occupational differences in this behavior? What sort of people eat together? Aside from family groups, are most groups segregated by age and sex? Which kind of customer eats the fastest? Which kind takes the longest? Do some individuals use this as a social event, or do all customers appear to be there strictly for the food? How do they treat the staff? Are there age, sex, or occupational differences in this treatment?

PROJECT 4: DOING AN EXPERIMENT

1. In this experiment, you can assess the effect of the physical attractiveness of children on adults' responses to them. The independent variable will be photographs of children who differ in attractiveness. A written statement about the child will be attached to the photograph—this description will be the same for all photos. The subjects will then be asked to answer questions about the child.

The first step is to develop the experimental manipulation. Obtain pictures of many children. These should all be the same sex and same apparent age. Now have three or four persons sort the pictures in terms of attractiveness. Record the ranks for each photo. Select two photos—one ranked attractive by all raters and one ranked unattractive by all raters. These two pictures will now be the experimental manipulation.

Develop the description that will accompany the pictures. The following description was adapted from a newspaper account of a child available for adoption:

> Three-year-old *David* is a solemn little *boy* who seems to carry the troubles of the world on *his* shoulders. But *his* mellow, sweet personality makes *him* a favorite of everyone who meets *him*. *He* has an amazing ability to put together Legos and *he's* good at games. *He* loves animals and they seem to love *him*. *He* plays better by *himself* than in groups, though *he* does fine with other children. *He'd* do best as part of a family where *his* quiet spirit won't be lost. (Words in italics have to be changed if pictures of female children are used.)

Now determine how you are going to measure the dependent variable. You might say that you are trying to assess the effectiveness of this type of adoption description and ask the subjects to rate the child on several scales:

Will David be adopted soon?

1____Very likely

2____

3____

4____

5____

6____

7____Very unlikely

How well will David adapt to a new family?
1____Very well
2____
3____
4____
5____
6____
7____Not at all well

How mature is David for his age?
1____Very immature
2____
3____
4____
5____
6____
7____Very mature

Will David have problems in school?
1____Very unlikely
2____
3____
4____
5____
6____
7____Very likely

Be sure to include a question that checks on the effectiveness of the manipulation:

Please rate this child in terms of physical attractiveness:
1____Very unattractive
2____
3____
4____
5____
6____
7____Very attractive

Since you will not be trying to generalize to a population, you may select your subjects in any way that is convenient. You should randomly assign each subject to an experimental condition. You might do this by flipping a coin—assign those with heads to condition 1 and those with tails to condition 2. You should have about 15 subjects in each experimental condition. Simply stop assigning subjects to a condition after you have reached the desired number.

Ask each subject to look at the picture and read the description. You could then interview the subject and fill in the questionnaire yourself. Or you could have the subject fill in the questionnaire. If you have appropriate equipment, you could have subjects enter their responses directly into a MicroCase data set using questionnaire data entry.

Then create a MicroCase data set and enter the data. Be sure to create a variable for the experimental condition—simply assign each subject a 1 or 2. You could then determine if there were differences in the dependent variables across the experimental conditions. Be sure to check that the experimental manipulation was effective—subjects perceived one child as more attractive than the other.

ALTERNATIVE EXPERIMENT: Do this same study using homely and attractive dogs.

2. Use similar procedures to replicate the study described in Chapter 6 in the textbook. That study examined the effect of a candidate's gender on voters' choices. In each condition, subjects were asked to read a description of a candidate. They were then asked a series of questions about the candidate. The only difference between the two conditions was the name of the candidate. In one condition, the candidate was clearly female and, in the other condition, the candidate was male.

First, create a description of a candidate. Since you want subjects to be aware of the gender of the candidate, you might use personal pronouns (he, his, him, she, hers, her) liberally. To create the two conditions, you need to select a female name and a male name. The apparent ethnicity of the names should be the same. For example, if the female name is Hispanic, then the male name should be Hispanic.

You then want to devise a way to measure the dependent variable. You might ask how likely subjects would be to vote for such a candidate, the extent to which they agree with the candidate's positions, and so on. Be sure to check the effectiveness of the manipulation. For example, after retrieving the description, you might ask them about various characteristics of the candidate, such as age, gender, and occupation.

After you enter data into a MicroCase data set, you can test the hypothesis that the gender of the candidate affects voters' preferences.

PROJECT 5: DOING CONTENT ANALYSIS

In the study described in Chapter 6, John C. Merrill reported the results of a content analysis of *Time* magazine stories on Presidents Truman, Eisenhower, and Kennedy. This project is based on that study.

The purpose of this study is to use content analysis to see if different magazines put their own "spin" on the behavior of the president. To obtain the multiple coders needed to check reliability in content coding, you might work with one or two classmates on this project, if your instructor approves. Otherwise, you will need to arrange for at least one coder in addition to yourself.

Select a current event in which the president was involved. Then you can go to the library and select several newspapers to compare. These might be from different parts of the country. Or you could select two news magazines or newspapers from different places on the political spectrum. For example, you might select one "mainstream" magazine such as *Time* or *Newsweek*, and a conservative magazine such as *The National Review* or a liberal magazine such as *The Nation*. Obtain from each publication stories on the selected event. Provide each coder with a copy of the stories, and ask him or her to identify each instance of bias and code it as positive or negative in the following categories:

1. *Attribution bias:* use of a "loaded" verb, such as "barked," "smiled," or "waffled," in place of a neutral verb, such as "said."
2. *Adjective bias:* use of a favorable or unfavorable adjective, such as "disorganized," "boring," "forceful," or "effective." These are subjective, or judgmental, adjectives, in contrast to objective, or neutral, adjectives, such as "blue" sky.
3. *Adverbial bias:* use of a favorable or unfavorable adverb, such as "warmly," "curtly," or "slyly." Frequently, these will be combined with attribution bias, such as in "chatted amiably" or "barked sarcastically."
4. *Outright opinion:* reaching a subjective conclusion rather than stating facts: "His inability to stay focused on the issue has confused his supporters as well as his opponents" or "His forceful presentation put his opponents on the defensive."
5. *Photographic bias:* portraying the president in a positive or negative manner in photographs or cartoons.

In tallying the codes, use only instances of bias on which all coders agree. If one coder cites an instance of negative bias that the other coders ignore, drop that instance. You can then compare the two magazines on each type of bias.

Appendix A:
Student Questionnaire

Please answer the following questions by placing a mark in the appropriate blank
or by writing in the requested information.

1. I really like science and math courses.
   - 1___Strongly agree
   - 2___Agree
   - 3___Disagree
   - 4___Strongly disagree

2. I am not sure that college is worth all the bother.
   - 1___Strongly agree
   - 2___Agree
   - 3___Disagree
   - 4___Strongly disagree

3. My career plans after I finish college are:
   - 1___Very definite
   - 2___Fairly clear
   - 3___At the "maybe" stage
   - 4___Still pretty much undecided

4. What is your present year in college?
   - 1___First
   - 2___Second
   - 3___Third
   - 4___Fourth
   - 5___Fifth or more

5. Do you live at home, in a dorm, or where?
   - 1___At home with my parent(s)
   - 2___In my own apartment or house
   - 3___In a dorm
   - 4___In a sorority
   - 5___In a fraternity

6. During an average week, how many hours do you spend studying for college?_____(write in number)

7. What is your GPA (Grade Point Average)?_____(write in number) If this is your first term in college, report your high school GPA.

8. Do you belong to a fraternity or sorority, whether as a pledge or as an active member?
   1___Yes
   2___No

9. If you had to choose between a course in literature or a course in science, which would you probably select?
   1___Literature
   2___Science

10. What is your age?_____

11. Have you ever received a ticket, or been charged by the police, for a traffic violation—other than illegal parking?
   1___Yes
   2___No

12. Were you ever picked up, or charged, by the police for any other reason, whether or not you were guilty?
   1___Yes
   2___No

13. Have you ever shoplifted?
   1___Yes
   2___No

14. Whether or not you ever have drunk alcoholic beverages such as liquor, wine, or beer, do you do so now or are you a total abstainer?
   1___Drink now
   2___Abstain now

15. Have you EVER tried marijuana?
   1___Yes, in the past year
   2___Yes, but not in the past year
   3___Never

16. Have you EVER tried cocaine (crack, rock, freebase)?
   1___Yes, in the past year
   2___Yes, but not in the past year
   3___Never

17. During the past year, have you been nauseated or vomited due to your drinking or drug use?

1___Yes

2___No

18. Have you ever cheated on an exam?

1___Yes, very often

2___Yes, quite often

3___Yes, a few times

4___Yes, but only once

5___No, not ever

19. IF you have ever cheated on an exam, was that in high school or in college?

1___In college

2___In high school

3___Both

20. Do you agree that people ought to have the right to end their own lives anytime they are tired of living?

1___Strongly agree

2___Agree

3___Disagree

4___Strongly disagree

21. Do you favor or oppose the death penalty for persons convicted of murder?

1___Favor

2___Oppose

Do you approve or disapprove of abortions under each of the following circumstances:

22. If the woman is not married and does not want to marry the man.

1___Approve

2___Disapprove

23. If the woman's own health is seriously endangered by the pregnancy.

1___Approve

2___Disapprove

24. If the woman is married but doesn't want any more children.

1___Approve

2___Disapprove

25. If the woman simply wants an abortion for any reason at all.

1___Approve

2___Disapprove

26. Do you smoke?
1___No
2___Yes

27. Do you have a computer?
1___Yes
2___No

Do you think the government ought to spend more or less money on each of the following:

28. On welfare?
1___Spend more
2___Spend less
3___Spend at the current level

29. On defense?
1___Spend more
2___Spend less
3___Spend at the current level

30. On space exploration?
1___Spend more
2___Spend less
3___Spend at the current level

31. On education?
1___Spend more
2___Spend less
3___Spend at the current level

32. The press often reports predictions about the future by people such as Jean Dixon, who claim to have psychic powers. Do you think some people do have such powers?
1___I am certain some people do have psychic powers.
2___I think some people probably have psychic powers.
3___I tend to doubt that anyone is a psychic.
4___I am certain this is all nonsense.

33. How much confidence do you place in astrology—the theory that the position of the stars and planets in relation to our birthdays has a lot to do with what we are like and what will happen to us?

1___A lot of confidence

2___Some confidence

3___Not much confidence

4___No confidence

34. Whom did you favor in the 1992 presidential election?

1___Bush

2___Clinton

3___Perot

4___Other

35. About how often do you attend religious services?

1___More than once a week

2___About once a week

3___At least once a month

4___At least twice a year

5___Seldom

6___Never

36. What is your religious preference?

1___Catholic

2___Protestant

3___Jewish

4___Other

5___None

37. Would you say that you are a religious person or that you are not?

1___Very religious

2___Somewhat religious

3___Not very religious

4___Not religious

38. When you were in high school, did you participate in an organized sport that involved competition with other schools?

1___Yes

2___No

39. Are you employed?

1___Yes, full-time

2___Yes, part-time

3___No

40. What is your current marital status?
   1___Single (never married)
   2___Married
   3___Divorced or separated
   4___Widowed

41. When you were 16, with whom were you living?
   1___Both parents
   2___One parent and a stepparent
   3___My mother
   4___My father
   5___Others

42. Thinking about your parents, or the people with whom you lived during high school, compared with other American families, would you say their income was below average or above?
   1___Far below average
   2___Below average
   3___Average
   4___Above average
   5___Far above average

43. Thinking about the home you lived in when you were in high school, about how many hardcover books were in the house?
   1___0–10
   2___11–25
   3___26–75
   4___76–100
   5___101–200
   6___201–500
   7___More than 500

44. What do you think is the ideal number of children for a family to have?
   0___None
   1___One
   2___Two
   3___Three
   4___Four
   5___Five
   6___Six or more

45. Race/ethnicity:
   1___White (Anglo)
   2___African American
   3___Asian American
   4___Hispanic American
   5___Native American
   6___Pacific Islander
   7___Other_____(write in)

46. Sex:
   1___Female
   2___Male

47. Were you born in the United States?
   1___Yes, in this state
   2___Yes, in another state
   3___No

48. Do you agree or disagree that a preschool child is likely to suffer if his or her mother works?
   1___Agree
   2___Disagree

49. It might be better for everyone if the husband takes care of earning a living and the wife takes care of the home and the children.
   1___Agree
   2___Disagree

50. Do you usually wear one or more rings on your fingers?
   1___Usually wear more than one ring
   2___Usually wear one ring
   3___Sometimes wear a ring
   4___Seldom wear a ring
   5___Never wear a ring

51. At present, do you have your own car?
   1___Yes
   2___No

52. If you had to be one or the other, would you rather be a dog or a cat?
   1___Dog
   2___Cat

53. Would you rate yourself as overweight, about right, or underweight?
    1___Quite overweight
    2___Somewhat overweight
    3___About right
    4___Somewhat underweight
    5___Quite underweight

54. How likely do you think it is that during your lifetime you will suffer a significant hair loss?
    1___Very likely
    2___Somewhat likely
    3___Not very likely
    4___Very unlikely

55. Have you ever used a sewing machine?
    1___Often
    2___Sometimes
    3___Once or twice
    4___Never

Please write in an answer to each of the following questions, estimating the answer to the best of your knowledge

56._____Estimate the world's total population (in billions).

57._____Estimate the percentage of the U.S. population who are African American.

58._____Estimate the percentage of Americans who are the victims of violent crime in any given year.

59._____Estimate the American family's median income in dollars per year.

60._____Estimate the percentage of Americans of voting age who voted in the 1992 presidential election.

61._____Estimate the percentage of the total popular vote received by Bill Clinton.

62._____Estimate the percentage of American adults who drink alcoholic beverages.

Appendix B: Codebooks

1) SEX
2) RACE
3) WH/AFRI.AM
4) MARITAL
5) REGION
6) AGE
7) OVER 50
8) WORKING?
9) URBAN?
10) PLACE SIZE
11) MOVERS
12) HUNT/FISH
13) FEAR WALK
14) ED YEARS
15) DEGREE
16) DAD PREST
17) INCOME @16
18) DAD DEGREE
19) MOM DEGREE
20) DAD EDUC!
21) MOM EDUC!
22) R.INCOME
23) INCOME
24) $ 50%50%
25) OWN HOME?
26) PHONE
27) EVER UNEMP
28) DRINK?
29) SOC. BAR

30) HAPPY?
31) EVER STRAY
32) SEX FREQ
33) # CHILDREN
34) # SIBS
35) SPANK?
36) POL. VIEW
37) POL.PARTY
38) VOTE IN 92
39) WHO IN 92?
40) CLINTON/NT
41) WOMAN PREZ
42) HELP HUSB
43) HOUSEWIFE
44) MEN BETTER
45) RELIGION
46) CH.ATTEND
47) HOW RELIG?
48) PRAY
49) GOV.MED.
50) MUCH GOV'T
51) SPACE PRG$
52) ENVIRON. $
53) HEALTH $
54) BIG CITY $
55) CRIME $
56) DRUGS $
57) EDUCATE $
58) BLACK $

59) DEFENSE $
60) FOR. AID $
61) WELFARE $
62) SPACE PR$2
63) ENVIRON.$2
64) HEALTH $2
65) BIG CITY$2
66) CRIME $2
67) DRUGS $2
68) EDUCATE $2
69) BLACK $2
70) DEFENSE $2
71) FOR. AID$2
72) WELFARE $2
73) ABORT DEF
74) ABORT WANT
75) ABORT HLTH
76) ABORT NO$
77) ABORT RAPE
78) ABORT SIGL
79) ABORT INDX
80) ATHEIST SP
81) RACIST SPK
82) COMMUN SPK
83) MILITI. SP
84) GAY SPEAK
85) FREE SPEAK
86) READ PAPER
87) WATCH TV

88) WATCH PBS?	110) ATTNDSPORT	132) RANDOM
89) HIT CHILD	111) VISIT ART	133) AGE!
90) HIT BEATER	112) AUTO RACE	134) PLACE SIZ!
91) HIT ROBBER	113) GARDEN	135) EDUCATION!
92) HIT OK?	114) DO SPORTS	136) DEGREE!
93) ATH. BOOK	115) VEGETARIAN	137) INCOME!
94) RACIST BK	116) MAN MADE	138) R.INCOME!
95) COMMI BOOK	117) ALL DIE	139) POL. VIEW!
96) MILIT BOOK	118) CANCER	140) POL.PARTY!
97) GAY BOOK	119) ORGANIC	141) CH.ATTEND!
98) BOOK INDEX	120) HEALTH	142) HOW RELIG!
99) BIG BAND	121) MOM WORK?	143) PRAY!
100) BLUEGRASS	122) FED.GOV'T?	144) GOV.MED!
101) CNTRY/WEST	123) SUP.COURT?	145) SEX FREQ!
102) MUSICALS	124) CONGRESS?	146) AGE AT WED
103) CLASSICAL	125) MILITARY?	147) STRICT REL
104) OPERA	126) EDUCATION?	148) VETERAN?
105) BLUES	127) COMPREHEND	149) HEALTH!
106) GOSPEL	128) ATTITUDE?	150) SAT.HEALT!
107) JAZZ	129) INTERMAR?	151) # SIBS!
108) RAP MUSIC	130) RACE SEG.	152) PUB.DECIDE
109) HVY METAL	131) ZODIAC	153) BUS.DECIDE

◆ SHORT LABEL: USA ◆

1) Case ID	18) DENSITY	35) ABORTION
2) POP 1990	19) CROWDED	36) ADOPTIONS
3) POP GO 90	20) MARRIAGE	37) WARM WINTR
4) % WHITE	21) DIVORCE	38) ELEVATION
5) % BLACK	22) %DIVORCED	39) AREA
6) % ASIAN	23) %M.DIVORCE	40) SOUTHNESS
7) %N.AMERICA	24) %F.DIVORCE	41) SO.ACCENTS
8) % HISPANIC	25) COUPLES	42) WESTNESS
9) MEXICAN K	26) % FEM.HEAD	43) REGION
10) P.RICAN K	27) MALE HOMES	44) COKE USERS
11) CUBAN K	28) %SINGLES	45) DRUG ED
12) IMMIGRANTS	29) %SINGLE M	46) ALCOHOL
13) AGE 5–17	30) %SINGLE F.	47) % WINE
14) % OVER 65	31) % WIDOWS	48) % BEER
15) AVER. AGE	32) % WIDOWERS	49) HEALTH IND
16) % RURAL	33) TEEN MOMS	50) AIDS DEATH
17) % METROPOL	34) % FEM.WORK	51) % FAT

52) SUICIDE	78) NEW HOMES	104) % BAPTIST
53) % FEM MD	79) % ON AFDC	105) CHURCH MEM
54) MDs	80) FOODSTAMPS	106) CRIME RATE
55) PLASTIC	81) $ PER CAP.	107) VIO.CRIME
56) SHRINKS	82) HOME VALUE	108) PROP.CRIME
57) CHIROPRACT	83) RENT	109) MURDER
58) PLAYBOY	84) P.TAX/CP	110) RAPE
59) #PLAYBOY	85) AUTOS PER	111) ROBBERY
60) MOTH.JONES	86) % POOR	112) ASSAULT
61) N.R./NAT.	87) % UNEMPLOY	113) BURGLARY
62) PEACE CORP	88) $ WORKERS	114) LARCENY
63) %FEMALE LG	89) % HIGH SCH	115) AUTO THEFT
64) ART $ PER	90) % COLLEGE	116) %BUSH 1988
65) ARC.DIGEST	91) DROPOUTS	117) %CLINTON92
66) CONNOISS'R	92) MATH SCORE	118) %BUSH '92
67) GOURMET	93) $PER PUPIL	119) %PEROT 92
68) COSMO	94) STU/TEACH	120) STATES '92
69) ROLLING ST	95) GRAD ED	121) FEM.LEGIS
70) PICKUPS	96) $ HIGH ED	122) LOBBYISTS
71) FLD&STREAM	97) % HIGH ED	123) BUSH88
72) HUNTING	98) COLLEGE $	124) CLINTON92
73) FISHING	99) LIBRARIES	125) FS$/PER
74) VETERANS	100) BOOK $	126) FS$/CAP
75) PUBLIC AID	101) %NO RELIG.	127) MILES/DRV.
76) HOMELESS	102) % JEWISH	128) MILES/VHCL
77) WELFARE $	103) % CATHOLIC	129) CARS/HSE90

◆ LONG LABEL: SURVEY ◆

1) SEX
RESPONDENT'S SEX

2) RACE
RESPONDENT'S RACE

3) WH/AFRI.AM
RACE (OTHER HAS BEEN CODED AS MISSING)

4) MARITAL
Are you currently—married, widowed, divorced, separated, or have you never been
married?

5) REGION
REGION OF INTERVIEW

6) AGE
RESPONDENT'S AGE GROUP

7) OVER 50
IS RESPONDENT OVER 50?

8) WORKING?
Last week were you working full time, part time, going to school, keeping house, or what?

9) URBAN?
INDIVIDUALS WHO REPORTED LIVING IN A BIG CITY, A SUBURB, OR A SMALL CITY
AND THOSE WHO REPORTED LIVING IN A VILLAGE OR THE COUNTRY

10) PLACE SIZE
Would you describe the place where you live as: 1) A big city; 2) The suburbs or outskirts of a
big city; 3) A small city or town; 4) A country village; 5) A farm or home in the country

11) MOVERS
When you were 16 years old, were you living in this same (city/town/county)?

12) HUNT/FISH
LAST 12 MONTHS DID YOU: Go hunting or fishing.

13) FEAR WALK
Is there any area right around here—that is, within a mile—where you would be afraid to walk
alone at night?

14) ED YEARS
Total years in school

15) DEGREE
HIGHEST EDUCATIONAL DEGREE EARNED BY RESPONDENT

16) DAD PREST
Prestige of father's occupation.

17) INCOME @16
Thinking about the time when you were 16 years old, compared with American families in general then, would you say your family income was—far below average, below average, average, above average, or far above average?

18) DAD DEGREE
HIGHEST EDUCATIONAL DEGREE OF RESPONDENT'S FATHER

19) MOM DEGREE
HIGHEST EDUCATIONAL DEGREE OF RESPONDENT'S MOTHER

20) DAD EDUC!
How many years of school did your father complete?

21) MOM EDUC!
How many years of school did your mother complete?

22) R.INCOME
In which of these groups did your earnings from (OCCUPATION) for last year fall? That is, before taxes or other deductions. Respondent's income on the 1991 survey.

23) INCOME
In which of these groups did your total family income, from all sources, fall last year before taxes, that is? Family income on the 1991 survey.

24) $ 50%50%
Family income on the 1991 survey divided into two equal groups.

25) OWN HOME?
(Do you/Does your family) own your (home/apartment), pay rent, or what?

26) PHONE
DOES RESPONDENT HAVE A TELEPHONE?

27) EVER UNEMP
At any time during the last ten years, have you been unemployed and looking for work for as long as a month?

28) DRINK?
Do you ever have occasion to use any alcoholic beverages such as liquor, wine, or beer, or are you a total abstainer?

29) SOC. BAR
HOW OFTEN: Go to a bar or tavern?

30) HAPPY?
Taken all together, how would you say things are these days—would you say that you are very happy, pretty happy, or not too happy?

31) EVER STRAY
Have you ever had sex with someone other than your husband or wife while you were married?

32) SEX FREQ
About how often did you have sex during the last 12 months?

33) # CHILDREN
How many children have you ever had? Please count all that were born alive at any time (including any you had from a previous marriage).

34) # SIBS
How many brothers and sisters did you have? Please count those born alive, but no longer living, as well as those alive now. Also include step-brothers and step-sisters, and children adopted by your parents.

35) SPANK?
Do you strongly agree, agree, disagree, or strongly disagree that it is sometimes necessary to discipline a child with a good, hard spanking?

36) POL. VIEW
I'm going to show you a scale on which the political views that people might hold are arranged from extremely liberal to extremely conservative. Where would you place yourself on this scale?

37) POL.PARTY
Generally speaking, do you usually think of yourself as a Republican, Democrat, Independent, or what?

38) VOTE IN 92
In 1992, you remember that Clinton ran for president on the Democratic ticket against Bush for the Republicans and Perot as an Independent. Do you remember for sure whether or not you voted in that election?

39) WHO IN 92?
IF VOTED: Did you vote for Clinton, Bush, or Perot?

40) CLINTON/NT
IF VOTED: Did you vote for Clinton, Bush, or Perot?

41) WOMAN PREZ
If your party nominated a woman for president, would you vote for her if she were qualified for the job?

42) HELP HUSB
It is more important for a wife to help her husband's career than to have one herself.

43) HOUSEWIFE
It is much better for everyone involved if the man is the achiever outside the home and the woman takes care of the home and family.

44) MEN BETTER
Most men are better suited emotionally for politics than are most women.

45) RELIGION
What is your religious preference? Is it Protestant, Catholic, Jewish, some other religion, or no religion?

46) CH.ATTEND
How often do you attend religious services?

47) HOW RELIG?
Would you call yourself a strong (RELIGIOUS PREFERENCE NAMED) or a not very strong (RELIGIOUS PREFERENCE NAMED)?

48) PRAY
About how often do you pray?

49) GOV.MED.
1) IT IS THE RESPONSIBILITY OF GOVERNMENT TO HELP 2) PEOPLE SHOULD TAKE CARE OF THEMSELVES

50) MUCH GOV'T
SCALE ON HOW MANY THINGS THE GOVERNMENT DOES: 1) I STRONGLY AGREE THAT GOVERNMENT SHOULD DO MORE TO 2) I STRONGLY AGREE THAT THE GOVERNMENT IS DOING TOO MUCH

51) SPACE PRG$
Spending on the space exploration program

52) ENVIRON. $
Spending on improving and protecting the environment

53) HEALTH $
Spending on improving and protecting the nation's health

54) BIG CITY $
Spending on solving the problems of the big cities

55) CRIME $
Spending on halting the rising crime rate

56) DRUGS $
Spending on dealing with drug addiction

57) EDUCATE $
Spending on improving the nation's education system

58) BLACK $
Spending on improving the conditions of Blacks

59) DEFENSE $
Spending on the military, armaments, and defense

60) FOR. AID $
Spending on foreign aid

61) WELFARE $
Are we spending too much, too little, or about the right amount on welfare?

62) SPACE PR$2
Spending on space exploration

63) ENVIRON.$2
Spending on the environment

64) HEALTH $2
Spending on health

65) BIG CITY$2
Spending on assistance to big cities

66) CRIME $2
Spending on law enforcement

67) DRUGS $2
Spending on drug rehabilitation

68) EDUCATE $2
Spending on education

69) BLACK $2
Spending on assistance to Blacks

70) DEFENSE $2
Spending on national defense

71) FOR. AID$2
Spending on assistance to other countries

72) WELFARE $2
Are we spending too much, too little, or about the right amount on assistance to the poor?

73) ABORT DEF
LEGAL ABORTION: If there is a strong chance of serious defect in the baby?

74) ABORT WANT
LEGAL ABORTION: If she is married and does not want any more children?

75) ABORT HLTH
LEGAL ABORTION: If the woman's own health is seriously endangered by the pregnancy?

76) ABORT NO$
LEGAL ABORTION: If the family has a very low income and cannot afford any more children?

77) ABORT RAPE
LEGAL ABORTION: If she became pregnant as a result of rape?

78) ABORT SIGL
LEGAL ABORTION: If she is not married and does not want to marry the man?

79) ABORT INDX
ABORTION INDEX: Sum of six abortion items

80) ATHEIST SP
Somebody who is against all churches and religion: If such a person wanted to make a speech in your (city/town/community) against churches and religion, should he be allowed to speak, or not?

81) RACIST SPK
If such a person wanted to make a speech in your community claiming that Blacks are inferior, should he be allowed to speak, or not?

82) COMMUN SPK
Suppose this admitted Communist wanted to make a speech in your community. Should he be allowed to speak, or not?

83) MILITI. SP
A person who advocates doing away with elections and letting the military run the country: If such a person wanted to make a speech in your community, should he be allowed to speak, or not?

84) GAY SPEAK
A man who admits that he is a homosexual: Suppose this admitted homosexual wanted to make a speech in your community. Should he be allowed to speak, or not?

85) FREE SPEAK
FREE SPEECH INDEX

86) READ PAPER
How often do you read the newspaper—every day, a few times a week, once a week, less than once a week, or never?

87) WATCH TV
On the average day, about how many hours do you personally watch television?

88) WATCH PBS?
How often do you watch programs shown on public television?

89) HIT CHILD
APPROVE AN ADULT MALE HITTING A STRANGER WHO: had hit the man's child after the child had accidentally damaged the stranger's car?

90) HIT BEATER
APPROVE AN ADULT MALE HITTING A STRANGER WHO: was beating up a woman and the man saw it?

91) HIT ROBBER
APPROVE AN ADULT MALE HITTING A STRANGER WHO: had broken into the man's house?

92) HIT OK?
Are there any situations that you can imagine in which you would approve of a man punching an adult male stranger?

93) ATH. BOOK
If some people in your community suggested that a book he wrote against churches and religion should be taken out of your public library, would you favor removing this book, or not?

94) RACIST BK
If some people in your community suggested that a book he wrote which said Blacks are inferior should be taken out of your public library, would you favor removing this book, or not?

95) COMMI BOOK
Suppose he wrote a book which is in your public library. Somebody in your community suggests that the book should be removed from the library. Would you favor removing it, or not?

96) MILIT BOOK
Suppose he wrote a book advocating doing away with elections and letting the military run the country. Somebody in your community suggests that the book be removed from the public library. Would you favor removing it, or not?

97) GAY BOOK
If some people in your community suggested that a book he wrote in favor of homosexuality should be taken out of your public library, would you favor removing this book, or not?

98) BOOK INDEX
BOOK INDEX (FREEDOM OF PRESS)

99) BIG BAND
LIKE MUSIC: Big Band/Swing

100) BLUEGRASS
LIKE MUSIC: Bluegrass

101) CNTRY/WEST
LIKE MUSIC: Country/Western

102) MUSICALS
LIKE MUSIC: Broadway musicals/show tunes

103) CLASSICAL
LIKE MUSIC: Classical music—symphony & chamber

104) OPERA
LIKE MUSIC: Opera

105) BLUES
LIKE MUSIC: Blues or Rhythm and Blues

106) GOSPEL
LIKE MUSIC: Gospel music

107) JAZZ
LIKE MUSIC: Jazz

108) RAP MUSIC
LIKE MUSIC: Rap music

109) HVY METAL
LIKE MUSIC: Heavy metal

110) ATTNDSPORT
LAST 12 MONTHS DID YOU: Attend an amateur or professional sports event?

111) VISIT ART
LAST 12 MONTHS DID YOU: Visit an art museum or gallery?

112) AUTO RACE
LAST 12 MONTHS DID YOU: Go to an auto, stock car, or motorcycle race?

113) GARDEN
LAST 12 MONTHS DID YOU: Grow vegetables, flowers, or shrubs in a garden?

114) DO SPORTS
LAST 12 MONTHS DID YOU: Participate in any sports activity such as softball, basketball, swimming, golf, bowling, skiing, or tennis?

115) VEGETARIAN
And how often do you refuse to eat meat for moral or environmental reasons?

116) MAN MADE
All radioactivity is made by humans.

117) ALL DIE
If someone is exposed to any amount of radioactivity, they are certain to die as a result.

118) CANCER
All pesticides and chemicals used on food crops cause cancer in humans.

119) ORGANIC
And how often do you make a special effort to buy fruits and vegetables grown without pesticides or chemicals?

120) HEALTH
Would you say your own health, in general, is excellent, good, fair, or poor?

121) MOM WORK?
Did your mother work for as long as a year after you were born and before you started first grade?

122) FED.GOV'T?
CONFIDENCE? Executive branch of the federal government.

123) SUP.COURT?
CONFIDENCE? U.S. Supreme Court.

124) CONGRESS?
CONFIDENCE? Congress.

125) MILITARY?
CONFIDENCE? Military.

126) EDUCATION?
CONFIDENCE? Education.

127) COMPREHEND
Was respondent's understanding of the questions good, fair, or poor?

128) ATTITUDE?
In general, what was the respondent's attitude toward the interview? Friendly, Cooperative, Impatient, or Hostile?

129) INTERMAR?
Do you think there should be laws against marriages between (Negroes/blacks) and whites?

130) RACE SEG.
White people have a right to keep (Negroes/Blacks) out of their neighborhoods if they want to, and (Negroes/Blacks) should respect that right.

131) ZODIAC
ASTROLOGICAL SIGN OF RESPONDENT

132) RANDOM
RANDOM NUMBER ASSIGNED TO EACH CASE

133) AGE!
RESPONDENT'S AGE

134) PLACE SIZ!
Would you describe the place where you live as... 1)A big city 2)The suburbs or outskirts of a big city 3)A small city or town 4)A country village 5)A farm or home in the country.

135) EDUCATION!
How many years of school did you complete?

136) DEGREE!
HIGHEST EDUCATIONAL DEGREE EARNED BY RESPONDENT

137) INCOME!
TOTAL ANNUAL FAMILY INCOME

138) R.INCOME!
RESPONDENT'S ANNUAL INCOME

139) POL. VIEW!
I'm going to show you a seven-point scale on which the political views that people might hold are arranged from extremely liberal to extremely conservative. Where would you place yourself on this scale?

140) POL.PARTY!
Generally speaking, do you usually think of yourself as a Republican, Democrat, Independent, or what?

141) CH.ATTEND!
How often do you attend religious services?

142) HOW RELIG!
Would you call yourself a strong (RELIGIOUS PREFERENCE NAMED) or a not very strong (RELIGIOUS PREFERENCE NAMED)?

143) PRAY!
About how often do you pray?

144) GOV.MED!
SCALE ON GOVERNMENT COVERING MEDICAL COSTS: 1) I STRONGLY AGREE IT IS THE RESPONSIBILITY OF GOVERNMENT TO HELP TO 5) I STRONGLY AGREE PEOPLE SHOULD TAKE CARE OF THEMSELVES

145) SEX FREQ!
About how often did you have sex during the last 12 months?

146) AGE AT WED
How old were you when you first married?

147) STRICT REL
Strictness of the Protestant denomination

148) VETERAN?
HAS RESPONDENT SERVED IN THE ARMED FORCES?

149) HEALTH!
Would you say your own health, in general, is excellent, good, fair, or poor?

150) SAT.HEALT!
How satisfied are you with your health and physical condition?

151) # SIBS!
How many brothers and sisters did you have? Please count those born alive, but no longer living, as well as those alive now. Also include step-brothers and step-sisters, and children adopted by your parents.

152) PUB.DECIDE

Select: 1)Government should let ordinary people decide for themselves how to protect the environment, even if it means that they don't always do the right thing, or 2)Government should pass laws to make ordinary people protect the environment, even if it interferes with people's right to make their own decisions.

153) BUS.DECIDE

Select: 1)Government should let businesses decide for themselves how to protect the environment, even if it means that they don't always do the right thing or 2) Government should pass laws to make businesses protect the environment, even if it interferes with businesses right to make their own decisions.

♦ LONG LABEL: USA ♦

1) Case ID

2) POP 1990
1990: POPULATION IN THOUSANDS (CENSUS)

3) POP GO 90
1980–90: PERCENT GROWTH (OR DECLINE) IN POPULATION (CENSUS)

4) % WHITE
1990: PERCENT WHITE (CENSUS)

5) % BLACK
1990: PERCENT BLACK (CENSUS)

6) % ASIAN
1990: PERCENT ASIAN (CENSUS)

7) %N.AMERICA
1990: PERCENT NATIVE AMERICAN (CENSUS)

8) % HISPANIC
1990: PERCENT HISPANIC—HISPANICS MAY BE OF ANY RACE (CENSUS)

9) MEXICAN K
1990: PERSONS OF MEXICAN ANCESTRY PER 1,000 POPULATION (CENSUS)

10) P.RICAN K
1990: PERSONS OF PUERTO RICAN ANCESTRY PER 1,000 (CENSUS)

11) CUBAN K
1990: PERSONS OF CUBAN ANCESTRY PER 1,000 (CENSUS)

12) IMMIGRANTS
1989: NEW IMMIGRANTS ADMITTED PER 10,000 POPULATION (SMAD, 1991)

13) AGE 5–17
1990: PERCENT OF POPULATION AGE 5–17 (CENSUS)

14) % OVER 65
1990: PERCENT OF THE POPULATION OVER AGE 65 (CENSUS)

15) AVER. AGE
1990: AVERAGE (MEAN) AGE OF THE POPULATION (CENSUS)

16) % RURAL
1990: PERCENT OF POPULATION LIVING IN RURAL AREAS—UNINCORPORATED
OR POPULATION LESS THAN 2,500 (CENSUS)

17) % METROPOL
1988: PERCENT OF THE POPULATION LIVING IN METROPOLITAN STATISTICAL
AREAS (S.A., 1990)

18) DENSITY
1990: POPULATION PER SQUARE MILE (CENSUS)

19) CROWDED
1990: PERCENT OF OCCUPIED HOUSING UNITS WITH MORE THAN 1 PERSON PER
ROOM (CENSUS)

20) MARRIAGE
1989: MARRIAGES PER 1,000 POPULATION (S.A., 1991)

21) DIVORCE
1989: DIVORCES PER 1,000 POPULATION (S.A., 1991)

22) %DIVORCED
1990: PERCENT OF THOSE 15 AND OVER WHO CURRENTLY ARE DIVORCED
(CENSUS)

23) %M.DIVORCE
1990: PERCENT OF MALES 15 AND OVER WHO CURRENTLY ARE DIVORCED
(CENSUS)

24) %F.DIVORCE
1990: PERCENT OF FEMALES 15 AND OVER WHO CURRENTLY ARE DIVORCED
(CENSUS)

25) COUPLES
1990: PERCENT OF HOUSEHOLDS OCCUPIED BY A MARRIED COUPLE (CENSUS)

26) % FEM.HEAD
1990: PERCENT OF HOUSEHOLDS OCCUPIED BY A WOMAN AND HER CHILDREN
(CENSUS)

27) MALE HOMES
1990: PERCENT OF HOUSEHOLDS WITHOUT AN ADULT FEMALE RESIDENT
(CENSUS)

28) %SINGLES
PERCENT OF PERSONS 15 AND OVER WHO HAVE NEVER BEEN MARRIED (CENSUS)

29) %SINGLE M
1990: PERCENT OF MALES 15 AND OVER WHO HAVE NEVER MARRIED (CENSUS)

30) %SINGLE F.
1990: PERCENT OF FEMALES AGE 15 AND OVER WHO HAVE NEVER MARRIED
(CENSUS)

31) % WIDOWS
1990: PROPORTION OF FEMALES AGE 15 AND OVER WHO CURRENTLY ARE
WIDOWS (CENSUS)

32) % WIDOWERS
1990: PERCENT OF MALES AGE 15 AND OVER WHO CURRENTLY ARE WIDOWERS
(CENSUS)

33) TEEN MOMS
1988: PERCENT OF ALL BIRTHS TO MOTHERS UNDER AGE 20 (S.P.R., 1991)

34) % FEM.WORK
1989: PERCENT OF ADULT FEMALES IN THE LABOR FORCE (SMAD, 1991)

35) ABORTION
1988: ABORTIONS PER 1,000 LIVE BIRTHS (S.A., 1991)

36) ADOPTIONS
1986: NUMBER OF ADOPTIONS PER 100,000 POPULATION (SMAD, 1991)

37) WARM WINTR
AVERAGE JANUARY LOW TEMPERATURE

38) ELEVATION
APPROXIMATE MEAN ELEVATION IN FEET

39) AREA
AREA IN SQUARE MILES

40) SOUTHNESS
DEGREES OF LATITUDE SOUTH OF THE NORTH POLE, BASED ON LOCATION OF STATE CAPITAL. NEW MEX. = COLO.; ARIZ. = UTAH. Omitted cases: Alaska, Hawaii.

41) SO.ACCENTS
1990: CIRCULATION OF SOUTHERN ACCENTS MAGAZINE PER 100,000 (ABC)

42) WESTNESS
DEGREE OF LATITUDE WEST OF PRIME MERIDIAN IS WESTERNMOST POINT OF STATE

43) REGION
CENSUS REGION

44) COKE USERS
1990: COCAINE ADDICTS PER 1,000 POPULATION (SENATE JUDICIARY COMMITTEE, USA TODAY, 8/6/90)

45) DRUG ED
1990: SCHOOL FUNDS PER STUDENT SPENT ON DRUG EDUCATION IN DOLLARS (SENATE JUDICIARY COMMITTEE, USA TODAY, 9/6/90)

46) ALCOHOL
1989: GALLONS OF ALCOHOLIC BEVERAGES CONSUMED PER PERSON 16 AND OVER (HCSR, 1993)

47) % WINE
1989: THE PERCENT OF ALCOHOLIC BEVERAGES CONSUMED THAT WAS WINE
(HCSR, 1993)

48) % BEER
1989: THE PERCENTAGE OF ALCOHOLIC BEVERAGES CONSUMED THAT WAS BEER
(HCSR, 1993)

49) HEALTH IND
STATE HEALTH RANKING AS CALCULATED BY NORTHWESTERN NATIONAL LIFE
INSURANCE CO. OF MINNEAPOLIS

50) AIDS DEATH
1991: TOTAL NUMBER OF AIDS DEATHS PER 100,000 THROUGH 1991 (HCSR, 1992)

51) % FAT
1990: PERCENT OF POPULATION 18 AND OVER WHO ARE OVERWEIGHT (MMWR,
DEC., 1991)

52) SUICIDE
1989: SUICIDES PER 100,000 (MVSR, 1/7/92)

53) % FEM MD
1990: PERCENT OF PHYSICIANS (M.D.s) WHO ARE FEMALE (HCSR, 1993)

54) MDs
1990: NUMBER OF PHYSICIANS (M.D.s) PER 100,000 (HCSR, 1993)

55) PLASTIC
1990: PLASTIC SURGEONS PER 100,000 (HCSR, 1993)

56) SHRINKS
1990: NUMBER OF PSYCHIATRISTS PER 100,000 (HCSR, 1993)

57) CHIROPRACT
1990: NUMBER OF CHIROPRACTORS PER 100,000 (HCSR, 1993)

58) PLAYBOY
1990: PLAYBOY CIRCULATION PER 100,000 POPULATION (ABC)

59) #PLAYBOY
1990: CIRCULATION OF PLAYBOY MAGAZINE (IN 1000S)

60) MOTH.JONES
1990: CIRCULATION OF MOTHER JONES MAGAZINE PER 100,000 POPULATION (ABC)

61) N.R./NAT.
1990: NATIONAL REVIEW CIRCULATION PER SUBSCRIBER TO THE NATION (ABC)

62) PEACE CORP
1985: TOTAL RESIDENTS WHO JOINED PEACE CORPS 1961–1985 PER 10,000 (THE PEACE CORPS, IN USA TODAY, 10/8/85)

63) %FEMALE LG
1991: PERCENT OF STATE LEGISLATORS WHO ARE FEMALE (S.P.R., 1991)

64) ART $ PER
1990: PER CAPITA STATE LEGISLATIVE APPROPRIATIONS FOR ARTS AGENCIES IN DOLLARS (S.A., 1991)

65) ARC.DIGEST
1990: CIRCULATION OF ARCHITECTURAL DIGEST (FINE HOMES) PER 100,000 (ABC)

66) CONNOISS'R
1990: CIRCULATION OF CONNOISSEUR MAGAZINE (ARTS, FINE LIVING) PER 100,000 (ABC)

67) GOURMET
1990: CIRCULATION OF GOURMET MAGAZINE (FINE FOOD) PER 100,000 (ABC)

68) COSMO
1990: CIRCULATION OF COSMOPOLITAN MAGAZINE PER 100,000 (ABC)

69) ROLLING ST
1990: CIRCULATION OF ROLLING STONE MAGAZINE PER 100,000 (ABC)

70) PICKUPS
1989: LIGHT TRUCKS (PICKUPS) PER 1,000 (HIGHWAY)

71) FLD&STREAM
1990: CIRCULATION OF FIELD & STREAM MAGAZINE PER 100,000 POPULATION (ABC)

72) HUNTING
1990: NUMBER OF RESIDENTS WHO PURCHASED HUNTING LICENSES PER 1,000 POPULATION (U.S. FISH & WILDLIFE)

73) FISHING
1990: NUMBER OF RESIDENTS WHO PURCHASED FISHING LICENSES PER 1,000 POPULATION (U.S. FISH & WILDLIFE)

74) VETERANS
1988: VETERANS PER 1,000 POPULATION (S.A. 1990)

75) PUBLIC AID
1990: PERCENT OF HOUSEHOLDS RECEIVING PUBLIC ASSISTANCE (CENSUS)

76) HOMELESS
1990: NUMBER OF HOMELESS PER 10,000 POPULATION (S.P.R., 9(9):13)

77) WELFARE $
1989: PER CAPITA STATE SPENDING ON WELFARE (SR, 1991)

78) NEW HOMES
1990: PERCENT OF ALL HOUSING UNITS CONSTRUCTED SINCE 1980 (CENSUS)

79) % ON AFDC
1988: PERCENT OF ALL HOUSEHOLDS RECEIVING AID TO FAMILIES WITH DEPENDENT CHILDREN (AFDC) (S.P.R., 1991)

80) FOODSTAMPS
1990: PERCENT OF POPULATION RECEIVING FOOD STAMPS (S.P.R., 1991)

81) $ PER CAP.
1987: PER CAPITA INCOME (S.A., 1991)

82) HOME VALUE
1990: MEDIAN VALUE OF OWNER-OCCUPIED HOUSING UNITS (CENSUS)

83) RENT
1990: MEDIAN MONTHLY RENT FOR RENTER-OCCUPIED HOUSING UNITS (CENSUS)

84) P.TAX/CP
1987: PROPERTY TAXES PER CAPITA

85) AUTOS PER
1989: AUTOMOBILES PER 1,000 (HIGHWAY STATISTICS, 1989)

86) % POOR
1990: PERCENT OF POPULATION BELOW OFFICIAL POVERTY LINE (CENSUS)

87) % UNEMPLOY
1991: PERCENT OF CIVILIAN LABOR FORCE UNEMPLOYED (E&E, 11/91)

88) $ WORKERS
1991: AVERAGE WEEKLY EARNINGS OF PRODUCTION WORKERS ON MANUFAC-
TURING PAYROLLS (E&E, 11/91)

89) % HIGH SCH
1990: PERCENT OF POPULATION 25 AND OLDER WHO HAVE COMPLETED HIGH
SCHOOL (CENSUS)

90) % COLLEGE
1990: PERCENT OF THE POPULATION 25 AND OLDER WHO HAVE A COLLEGE
DEGREE (CENSUS)

91) DROPOUTS
1990: PERCENT OF PERSONS WHO LEFT SCHOOL WITHOUT GRADUATING FROM
HIGH SCHOOL (WA, 1993)

92) MATH SCORE
1991: AVERAGE MATH PROFICIENCY SCORES BY 8TH GRADERS (USA TODAY,
6/7/91)

93) $PER PUPIL
1989–90: ANNUAL EXPENDITURES PER PUPIL FOR PUBLIC ELEMENTARY AND
SECONDARY SCHOOLS (CHRON, 1991)

94) STU/TEACH
1989: AVERAGE NUMBER OF STUDENTS PER TEACHER IN PUBLIC ELEMENTARY
AND SECONDARY SCHOOLS (CHRON, 1991)

95) GRAD ED
1990: PERCENT OF PERSONS 25 AND OLDER WITH AN ADVANCED DEGREE
(CENSUS)

96) $ HIGH ED
1990: PER CAPITA LOCAL AND STATE GOVERNMENT SPENDING FOR HIGHER
EDUCATION (CENSUS)

97) % HIGH ED
1990: PERCENT OF STATE AND LOCAL SPENDING GOING TO HIGHER EDUCATION
(CENSUS)

98) COLLEGE $
1990: AVERAGE UNDERGRADUATE COSTS (TUITION, FEES, BOARD & ROOM) AT
PUBLIC INSTITUTIONS (DIGEST, 1991)

99) LIBRARIES
1989: PUBLIC LIBRARIES (AND BRANCHES) PER 10,000 (S.R., 1992)

100) BOOK $
1987: PER CAPITA RETAIL SALES BY BOOKSTORES (CENSUS OF RETAIL TRADE, 1987)

101) %NO RELIG.
1990: PERCENT OF THE POPULATION WHO SAY THEY HAVE NO RELIGION
(KOSMIN)

102) % JEWISH
1990: PERCENT OF THE POPULATION WHO GIVE THEIR RELIGIOUS PREFERENCE
AS JEWISH (KOSMIN)

103) % CATHOLIC
1990: PERCENT OF THE POPULATION WHO GIVE THEIR RELIGIOUS PREFERENCE
AS CATHOLIC (KOSMIN)

104) % BAPTIST
1990: PERCENT OF THE POPULATION WHO GIVE THEIR RELIGIOUS PREFERENCE
AS BAPTIST (KOSMIN)

105) CHURCH MEM
1990: PERCENT OF POPULATION BELONGING TO A LOCAL CHURCH

106) CRIME RATE
1992: TOTAL INDEX CRIMES PER 100,000 (UCR, 1993)

107) VIO.CRIME
1992: TOTAL VIOLENT CRIMES PER 100,000 (UCR, 1993)

108) PROP.CRIME
1992: TOTAL PROPERTY CRIMES PER 100,000 (UCR, 1993)

109) MURDER
1992: HOMICIDES PER 100,000 POPULATION (UCR)

110) RAPE
1992: RAPES PER 100,000 (UCR, 1993)

111) ROBBERY
1992: ROBBERIES PER 100,000 (UCR, 1993)

112) ASSAULT
1992: ASSAULTS PER 100,000 (UCR, 1992)

113) BURGLARY
1992: BURGLARIES PER 100,000 (UCR, 1993)

114) LARCENY
1993: LARCENIES PER 100,000 (UCR, 1993)

115) AUTO THEFT
1992: MOTOR VEHICLES STOLEN PER 100,000 POPULATION (UCR, 1993)

116) %BUSH 1988
1988: PERCENT OF TWO-PARTY VOTE WON BY GEORGE BUSH (REPUBLICAN) (WA, 1993)

117) %CLINTON92
1992: PERCENT OF VOTES FOR CLINTON (DEM.) (WA, 1993)

118) %BUSH '92
1992: PERCENT OF THE VOTES FOR BUSH (REP.) (WA, 1993)

119) %PEROT 92
1992: PERCENT OF VOTES FOR PEROT (INDEP.) (WA, 1993)

120) STATES '92
1992: DARK STATES CARRIED BY CLINTON, LIGHT STATES CARRIED BY BUSH (WA, 1993)

121) FEM.LEGIS
1993: PERCENT WOMEN IN STATE LEGISLATURES (from the Center for the American Woman and Politics)

122) LOBBYISTS
1991: NUMBER OF REGISTERED LOBBYISTS PER STATE LEGISLATOR (S.R.)

123) BUSH88
STATES CARRIED BY BUSH (DARK); BY DUKAKIS (LIGHT) IN 1988 PRESIDENTIAL
ELECTION

124) CLINTON92
STATES CARRIED BY CLINTON (DARK); BUSH (LIGHT) IN 1992 PRESIDENTIAL
ELECTION

125) FS$/PER
1993: AVERAGE YEARLY FOOD STAMP BENEFIT FOR INDIVIDUAL RECIPIENT (SA, 1995)

126) FS$/CAP
1993: ANNUAL COST OF FOOD STAMP BENEFITS PER CAPITA (TOTAL POPULATION)
(SA, 1995)

127) MILES/DRV.
1993: ANNUAL VEHICLE MILES PER DRIVER (HIGHWAY)

128) MILES/VHCL
1993: ANNUAL MILES PER VEHICLE (HIGHWAY)

129) CARS/HSE90
1990: VEHICLES AVAILABLE PER OCCUPIED HOUSING UNIT

◆ SOURCES ◆

The sources of each variable in the **USA** data file is indicated in its long label. Often these are abbreviated. A complete key to these abbreviations follows.

ABC: Audit Bureau of Circulation *Blue Book*

CENSUS: The summary volumes of the 1990 U.S. Census

CHRON.: *The Chronicle of Higher Education Almanac*

DIGEST: *Digest of Education Statistics*

E&E: *Employment and Earnings*, U.S. Bureau of Labor Statistics

HCSR: *Health Care State Rankings*, Morgan Quitno

HIGHWAY: *Highway Statistics*, U.S. Department of Transportation

KOSMIN: Kosmin, Barry A. 1991 *Research Report: The National Survey of religious Identification*, New York: CUNY Graduate Center.

MMWR: *Morbidity and Mortality Weekly Report*, Centers for Disease Control

MVSR: *Monthly Vital Statistics Report*, Centers for Disease Control

S.A.: *Statistical Abstract of the United States*

SMAD: *State and Metropolitan Area Data Book*, 1991

S.P.R.: *State Policy Reference*

SR: *State Rankings*, Morgan Quitno

UCR: *The Uniform Crime Reports*

WA: World Almanac

LICENSE AGREEMENT

READ THIS LICENSE AGREEMENT CAREFULLY BEFORE OPENING THE DISKETTE PACKAGE. BY OPENING THIS PACKAGE YOU ACCEPT THE TERMS OF THE AGREEMENT.

MicroCase® Corporation, hereinafter called the Licensor, grants the purchaser of this software package, hereinafter called the Licensee, the right to use and reproduce the following software: *Social Research Using MicroCase* in accordance with the following terms and conditions.

Permitted Uses

◆ You may use this software only for educational purposes.

◆ You may use the software on any compatible computer, provided the software is used on only one computer and by one user at a time.

◆ You may make a backup copy of the diskette(s).

Prohibited Uses

◆ You may not use this software for any purposes other than educational purposes.

◆ You may not make copies of the documentation or program disk, except backup copies as described above.

◆ You may not distribute, rent, sub-license or lease the software or documentation.

◆ You may not alter, modify, or adapt the software or documentation, including, but not limited to, translating, decompiling, disassembling, or creating derivative works.

◆ You may not use the software on a network, file server, or virtual disk.

THIS AGREEMENT IS EFFECTIVE UNTIL TERMINATED. IT WILL TERMINATE IF LICENSEE FAILS TO COMPLY WITH ANY TERM OR CONDITION OF THIS AGREEMENT. LICENSEE MAY TERMINATE AT ANY OTHER TIME BY DESTROYING THE SOFTWARE TOGETHER WITH ALL COPIES. IF THIS AGREEMENT IS TERMINATED BY LICENSOR, LICENSEE AGREES EITHER TO DESTROY OR RETURN THE ORIGINAL AND ALL EXISTING COPIES OF THE SOFTWARE TO THE LICENSOR WITHIN FIVE (5) DAYS AFTER RECEIVING NOTICE OF TERMINATION FROM THE LICENSOR.

MicroCase Corporation retains all rights not expressly granted in this License Agreement. Nothing in the License Agreement constitutes a waiver of MicroCase Corporation's rights under U. S. copyright laws or any other Federal or State Law.

Should you have any questions concerning this Agreement, you may contact MicroCase Corporation by writing to: MicroCase Corporation, 1301 120th Avenue N.E., Bellevue, WA 98005, ATTN: College Publishing Division.